DATE DUE

MAY 2 3 1992	JUN 0 5 1994	
	DEC 0 4 2000	
DEC 1 9 1992	MAY 0 7 2002	
FEB 0 3 1996	JUN 0 2 2003	
MAR 2 4 1996		
FEB 1 7 1998		
OCT 0 3 1998		

DEMCO 38-296

Modern Critical Interpretations

James Joyce's
Dubliners

Modern Critical Interpretations

James Joyce's
Dubliners

Edited and with an introduction by

Harold Bloom
Sterling Professor of the Humanities
Yale University

Chelsea House Publishers ◊ *1988*
NEW YORK ◊ NEW HAVEN ◊ PHILADELPHIA

© 1988 by Chelsea House Publishers,
a division of Chelsea House Educational Communications, Inc.

Introduction © 1988 by Harold Bloom

Printed and bound in the United States of America

10 9 8 7 6 5 4 3 2 1

∞ The paper used in this publication meets the minimum
requirements of the American National Standard for Permanence
of Paper for Printed Library Materials, Z39.48–1984.

Library of Congress Cataloging-in-Publication Data
James Joyce's Dubliners / edited and with an introduction by Harold Bloom.
     p.   cm.—(Modern critical interpretations)
   Bibliography: p.
   Includes index.
   Summary: A collection of eleven critical essays about Joyce's
collection of stories, arranged chronologically in the order of
their original publication.
   ISBN   1-55546-019-4 (alk. paper): $24.50
   1. Joyce, James, 1882–1941. Dubliners. [1. Joyce, James,
1882–1941. Dubliners. 2. English literature—Irish authors—
History and criticism.] I. Bloom, Harold. II. Series.
PR6019.09D875   1988
823'.912—dc19

Contents

Editor's Note

This book gathers together a representative selection of the best modern critical interpretations of James Joyce's classic book of short stories, *Dubliners*. The critical essays are reprinted here in the chronological order of their original publications. I am grateful to Onno Oerlemans and Paul Barickman for their assistance in editing this volume.

My introduction analyzes the story "Eveline" as a negation of a Paterian "privileged moment" or "epiphany," as Joyce called it in *Stephen Hero*. Robert Adams Day begins the chronological sequence of criticism with a consideration of Lenehan in "Two Gallants," who is seen as possessing both a realistic and a mythic identity.

In a study of the imagery of virginity in "The Dead," Tilly Eggers shows us that Joyce did not fix any single role on women, while Phillip Herring's reading of "The Sisters" emphasizes the indirection of Joyce's anti-clericalism in that story. Mary T. Reynolds subtly traces a Dantesque pattern that allies *Dubliners* to the moral structure of the *Inferno*.

The contexts of *Dubliners*, cultural and historical, are illuminated by Hugh Kenner, after which John Paul Riquelme denies the supposedly Flaubertian impersonality of Joyce as a narrative presence in the book.

Writing on "A Painful Case," Lindsey Tucker rescues the story as a vision of art as integrative process. "The Dead" returns with Ross Chambers's estimate of Gabriel Conroy as an ambivalent portrait of the artist, embodying an idea of order but unable to love. Fritz Senn, noted Swiss Joycean, reads "The Boarding House" as a "love story of wrong turnings."

"Ivy Day in the Committee Room" receives a Nietzschean analysis by Thomas B. O'Grady, who reflects upon Joyce's vision of his countrymen as being helplessly trapped in the nightmare of history. Margot Norris concludes this volume with a discussion of "Clay," which she judges to possess the ambivalent rhetorical purposes of both mocking and aggrandizing its protagonist, Maria.

Introduction

Joyce's scholars have studied the relation of *Dubliners* to its principal precursors: the fictions of Flaubert and Chekhov. There is a more complex relation, because more negative, to the vision of Walter Pater. The Paterian epiphany, turned inside out, is transformed by Joyce into the negative moments of *Dubliners*. *Dubliners,* an admirable and unified collection of short stories, is a more mixed work aesthetically than much criticism of Joyce acknowledges. "After the Race" is a weak story, and "An Encounter" and "Araby" do not reread well. But "Ivy Day in the Committee Room" is rightly and universally judged a masterpiece, and "The Dead," by common consent, inaugurates the art of the mature Joyce. I will confine myself here to the slight yet remarkable story "Eveline" in order to ponder one of Joyce's negative moments, his emptied-out version of the Paterian flare of radiance against darkening backgrounds.

"Eveline," when first read, seems a story by George Moore, who like the early Joyce was much influenced by Flaubert. Repeated readings show how subtle, and poignantly ambivalent the story becomes. If Joyce's Dublin is, as he asserted, "the centre of paralysis," then poor Eveline is presumably a victim of that paralysis, since we are to believe that she does care for Frank, her sailor lover. I would suppose that he is sincere, despite the doubts expressed by that shrewd ironist Hugh Kenner, who points out that the ship undoubtedly has Liverpool, rather than Buenos Aires, as its destination. But I do not think it much matters whether Frank is a deceiver, as Kenner believes, or whether Eveline and Frank are going to Liverpool in order to sail from there to Argentina. What seems clear is that a sailor fifty times more plausible than Frank would not budge the pathetic Eveline, who is a victim of her nation, her religion, her father, and finally of herself.

Eveline's mother, bullied and beaten by her dreadful father, died

1

in madness, constantly uttering corrupt Gaelic variously interpreted by Joyce scholars as "the end of pleasure is pain" or "the end of song is raving madness." By her final failure of nerve, Eveline seems to forfeit pleasure and song, while continuing towards what is going to be pain and raving madness anyway. She will be vulnerable to an Irish version of the return of the repressed, which means that she will end in violence, presumably towards herself. Joyce's lasting heritage to Western literature appears to be his suspension of the will, both in his protagonists and in the author. Authorial suspension of the will, whether in Wordsworth or in Joyce, is itself a fiction and is less interesting, in *Dubliners,* than the will-lessness of Eveline and her fellow residents of the Irish capital. The Joycean epiphany, like the Paterian privileged moment, never comes to those who desire or choose it. Suddenly it is there, and descends upon one with total authority, negating personality and hope, in Joyce's negative version:

> She stood among the swaying crowd in the station at the North Wall. He held her hand and she knew that he was speaking to her, saying something about the passage over and over again. The station was full of soldiers with brown baggages. Through the wide doors of the sheds she caught a glimpse of the black mass of the boat, lying in beside the quay wall, with illumined portholes. She answered nothing. She felt her cheek pale and cold and, out of a maze of distress, she prayed to God to direct her, to show her what was her duty. The boat blew a long mournful whistle into the mist. If she went, to-morrow she would be on the sea with Frank, steaming toward Buenos Ayres. Their passage had been booked. Could she still draw back after all he had done for her? Her distress awoke a nausea on her body and she kept moving her lips in silent fervent prayer.
>
> A bell clanged upon her heart. She felt him seize her hand:
> —Come!
>
> All the seas of the world tumbled about her heart. He was drawing her into them: he would drown her. She gripped with both hands at the iron railing.
> —Come!
>
> No! No! No! It was impossible. Her hands clutched the iron in frenzy. Amid the seas she sent a cry of anguish!
> —Eveline! Evvy!

He rushed beyond the barrier and called to her to follow. He was shouted at to go on but he still called to her. She set her white face to him, passive, like a helpless animal. Her eyes gave him no sign of love or farewell or recognition.

You could say that Eveline Hill is shaped so as to be the antithesis of Nora Barnacle, a lady so tough that the negative moments remained external to her. Wretched Eveline *is* a perpetually negative moment, monument to Dublin repression. But that is not precise enough. What Eveline experiences, at her story's end, is more than the disabling psychic defense of isolation, in which all context is burned away, and more even than the estranging consequences of hysteria. What descends upon her is not less than a vastation: sight is reduced to mass and color, nausea and prayer become intermixed, and all affect is an ocean, in which she must drown. The story's weakest sentence allows Joyce to be too judgmental: "She set her white face to him, passive, like a helpless animal." Eveline, as Joyce has represented her, is neither passive nor a helpless animal. Joyce makes a great recovery, worthy of him, in the final sentence: "Her eyes gave him no sign of love or farewell or recognition." She has no will and, in this negative moment, almost no consciousness. What paralyzes her is what Joyce called the moral history of his city and his nation, a history for which he held the Church responsible. "Silent fervent prayer" in this passage becomes a metaphor of death-in-life. Wordsworth, visionary of the positive epiphany, said of his spots of time that they gave precise knowledge of the extent to which the mind was lord and master, with outward sense the servant of the mind's creative will. "Eveline" represents the negation of Wordsworthianism and of its novelistic descendants in George Eliot and Henry James. Joyce shows us the triumph of outward sense, or the power of the universe of death over the victimized mind of the Dubliner, Eveline Hill.

Joyce's Gnomons, Lenehan, and the Persistence of an Image

Robert Adams Day

Our understanding of characters and characterization in the novel has vastly increased in sophistication since the days when it was possible to ask seriously how many children Lady Macbeth had, or to see characters as mere portraits of the author and his friends or enemies, or to view them functionally as foils or *ficelles* and not much more. Even so, human nature being what it is, we must struggle continually against the temptation to forget that novels like poems are verbal structures merely; or that, reversing our angle of vision, our knowledge of Jesus or of Napoleon is in one very important sense exactly like our knowledge of Hamlet: it is ultimately derived entirely from reading words written or printed—arbitrary symbolic data representing conceptual reductions of sense—data.

I want to discuss a few of the printed data that can be discovered and shown concerning a minor character of Joyce's, Lenehan—who has no given name like real people. The aggregate of these printed data can lead us into some unorthodox but instructive ways of examining the conception and genesis of "character" in the mind of Joyce and perhaps of other writers as well, for Lenehan bears about him traces of his creation, and achieves a very strange kind of immortality.

The more specialized criticism dealing with Joyce's characters and characterization has developed in lines parallel with those followed by criticism in general. Thus his characters have been seen as though they were real persons now living, therefore possessing a theoretically infinite

From *Novel: A Forum on Fiction* 14, no. 1 (Fall 1980). ©1980 by Novel Corp.

store of recoverable data: how many lovers had Molly Bloom, and should we like to be married to her? Stephen Dedalus in the *Portrait* is the young Joyce, perhaps painted by Picasso or Braque; Molly Bloom is an amalgam of Nora Joyce and the Virgin Mary. But we have also had ingenious and elaborate psychoanalytic studies of Joyce's figures; semiotic and structural purifications of them into patterns that permit comparative analysis; and other approaches, less easy to label, such as that in a recent volume which takes the position that Joyce's characterization "is predicated upon the coexistence (not the resolution) of opposites," and that the Joycean character is constituted, having an unknowable "soul," by surrounding it with collocations of details, stylistic and other, which as it were give the shape of the invisible entity within. The characters have also been seen as in a sense projections of Joyce himself, but in a mode far more subtle and therefore perhaps more truly Joycean than those envisaged by earlier scholars. I propose to follow a method which is writer- rather than reader-oriented; which in various ways resembles some of the last-mentioned approaches; but which, rather than dwelling on the great triad of Stephen, Bloom, and Molly, as nearly all critics have done, considers how Lenehan, a very minor character indeed, grew in Joyce's mind. If his ingredients on examination turn out to be bizarre, perhaps the greater figures past whom he flits may get additional illumination from him.

If we follow the simpler, older, or less sophisticated approaches, Lenehan is a character in the *Dubliners* story "Two Gallants" and a minor character in *Ulysses*. Parasite, toady, sponger, jackal, he is vivid, pathetic, believable; most of us have known him in real life, and so we are tempted in discussing him to add data that are not on Joyce's pages. Second, like the *Dubliners* character Little Chandler, Lenehan is a projection of a part of Joyce, a person whom Joyce might have become had he not met Nora, left Dublin, and become a dedicated artist; Joyce used traits of Mick Hart and Matthew Kane, Dubliners he knew, to create him, and took his name from a reporter on the *Irish Times;* if he has a literary ancestry at all, he may be a degenerate modern version of Chaucer's hospitable Franklin. Lastly, Lenehan acts as confidant to the repulsive character Corley in "Two Gallants," and in his flittings in and out of *Ulysses* he enriches the cast of characters. He replays his part of jackal with Blazes Boylan, he is seen in the newspaper office, on the streets, in the Ormond Hotel, in the pub, at the maternity hospital; he gives Boylan the worthless tip on the horse Sceptre for the Ascot Gold Cup, and derides Bantam Lyons, who was about to bet on the winning horse Throwaway; and there are hints that he may have been one of Molly's lovers in the past. In sort, a perfectly respectable (in the artistic sense) minor character, and what more is there to say of him?

There is a good deal. Lenehan gives us a new and very basic insight into what "character" really means to Joyce; he can lead us to a cosmology of Joyce's imaginative universe as recreated in art, and to an astonishing view of how important apparently trivial objects and gestures can be in that universe. Lenehan tells us that Joyce's cosmos is more nearly like that of William Blake than anything else, and that among its most important inhabitants are gnomons. "Lenehan" is nothing more than a name bestowed in deference to conventional realism on an agglomeration of gnomons at two points in their mythical history. (Parenthetically one might point out that that any eminent name that one likes to consider is but a label given to an agglomeration of atoms at a point in *their* history.)

"Blakean universe" and "gnomon" require definition. Blake, like Joyce, spent his life writing the book of himself, as Joyce clearly recognized. Both thought in archetypes, for which I shall use Carl Jung's definition, "a kind of readiness to produce over and over again the same or similar mythical ideas" (*Symbols of Transformation,* trans. R. F. C. Hull). The total work of each is a whole, in which each part reflects and therefore in a sense *is* the whole, and is in transformed terms a version or retelling of each and every other part. The life of Blake or Joyce is also the history of the human mind and of each mind, the history of the universe, the life of God or Christ or Satan or John Smith, the history of human kind and the life of any or Everyman, and of the processes of psychology according to any school of analysis. This cosmos, however, operates in space as well as time, so that geographical location corresponds with existence at a date in history; movement is the same as growing old or young. But while it is easy for us to say that everything is everything else and at the same time and everywhere, and think that we grasp the concept, it leads to paradoxes which Joyce and Blake easily handled, but which make our imaginations boggle unless we can be at ease, say, with the mystery of the Trinity; and it quite destroys any conventional notion of "character." The relevant paradox for our purpose is this: each self is at once itself and a part of itself and all the other parts of itself; in Joyce's own words, "Each . . . is so to say one person although it is composed of persons—as Aquinas relates of the heavenly hosts." To dramatize all this is something of a problem; and this is why Blake pretends to be writing about Los and Urthona and Bowlahoola and Golgonooza and why Joyce finally wrote *Finnegans Wake*. Mythical personages and ideas are free from the petty trammels of space, time, and identity; they can live at once in them and out of them.

The fundamental importance of Blake's vision in forming Joyce's has been well documented, and few will quarrel with the notion of *Finnegans Wake*, at least, as a Blakean universe. But Joyce was thinking mythically, in images and archetypes, from the beginning, and in all his books before the *Wake* a ghost of the Blakean cosmos lurks, very faint at first, but materializing ever more thickly. Lenehan inhabits it. Like Lewis Carroll's Cheshire cat (the best simile that presents itself) he is at first a grin without a cat, then a cat without a grin (in *Dubliners* and *Ulysses*, where he has a name as well as a local habitation), and then, in the *Wake*, gathered into the artifice of eternity, he is again a grin without a cat. The grin consists of objects and gestures at once veristic and emblematic, and these are Lenehan's gnomons.

"Gnomons," with "simony" and "paralysis," is one of the three words that fascinate the little boy in the first story of *Dubliners*, and like them it has been subjected to some very fantastic manipulations in an effort to see it as a key to Joyce's art. It is true that "in the Euclid," as the boy says, a gnomon is that part of a parallelogram which remains after a similar parallelogram has been taken from one of its corners—a sort of drunken letter L; but that information does not take us very far. If instead we have recourse, as Joyce so often did, to Skeat's *Etymological Dictionary*, where "gnomon" lives close to the very Joycean word "gorbellied," we find that a gnomon is the index of a dial, that is, a pointer, from the Greek word meaning an interpreter, one who knows. If we suppose that Joyce thought simultaneously of a gnomon as an indicator and as an interpreter who knows, we may connect this notion with two favorite doctrines of his: first, the doctrine of signatures, telling us that the appearances of things are hieroglyphics of their nature and that heavenly things are reflected in the things of earth, and second, the tradition of emblems of efficacy, which also tells of heavenly truths. In the early ages of the Church such emblems told the illiterate who a saint was and what he was good for; thus the patron of pedagogues might well be St. Cassian, whose pagan pupils pierced him with styluses and beat in his skull with tablets. Joyce had good fun with such emblems in "Cyclops," but they also had a serious purpose for him, as with Bloom's symbolic potato, Molly's roses, Stephen's ashplant, Mulligan's gold teeth (like a saint he is called

"Chrysostomos," Cranly's "iron crown" of hair and eating of figs (he is equated with John the Baptist). Perhaps every character in Joyce is not equipped with gnomons, but Lenehan certainly is. Indeed, under the aspect of eternity or of Blake he is an immortal icon—a collection of symbolic objects, a name, certain mythic functions—who becomes the literary equivalent of incarnate only in the more realistic fictions, but who repeats the same functions eternally on the mythic level.

If this theory is valid we can always detect the presence of "Lenehan" if we see even one of the objects or gestures that are his pointers, emblems, or gnomons, and we can be sure that the idea or process he represents is going on; he is at once a fictional character, a *figura* in Joycean typology, and a state, condition, or activity in the informing myth. He is always a betrayer or rather an assistant at a betrayal—a Judas who helps the evil conqueror to vanquish the defenceless hero. But in Joycean myth this process is inevitable and, though painful, necessary; to explain by analogy, the Romans could not have crucified Christ and thus enabled him to perform the necessary redemption of mankind without the cooperation of Judas. This paradox of the evil-yet-good betrayer is always very clear to Joyce, for in his Blakean universe the hero always invites and even arranges his own betrayal, and the betrayer is always in some way a part of the hero's being.

In its most purified form and relevant archetype in the Joycean universe is this. A male figure generates and forms a female figure for his possession, enjoyment, comfort, and fulfillment. But she necessarily leans toward infidelity, and a male figure of evil from outside seduces her, defiles her, abducts her, or somehow renders her helpless and useless. But just as a vampire cannot first enter a house without an invitation, a catalyst is needed; and a minor male figure, also generated by the hero-figure, opens the gates to the invader. Thus the hero betrays himself.

Blake's "Mental Traveller," which Joyce knew well from the Yeats-Ellis edition, offers in its vision of the way life goes in the fallen world perhaps the most striking and concrete analogue to this archetype, and may elucidate it for the reader. Perceived through the eyes of a traveller from Eternity, a male Babe is fed upon and tortured by a "Woman Old" while "she grows young as he grows old." The situation of vampirism is then reversed as he has become strong and she helpless; she is reborn from fire as a sort of Muse, and he in feeble age turns to an earthly Maiden who supportively leads him astray. The cycle endlessly repeats itself, even though the appearance and behavior of the two figures may superficially alter; one sex always preys upon the other, deriving nourishment and rejuvenation from destroying the other's life. Only the seer or artist, by embracing the frighteningly glorious Muse-figure, might escape the cycle.

Joyce, like Blake, contrived a myth that could be as large or small as one liked. William Blake, the city of London, the British Isles, the world, the universe, secular history, sacred history, the life of the human mind, and the drama enacted by the giant Albion or by his dispersed fragments are all one, and Blake may refer to all their stories by depicting an incident or mentioning a name in the story of any one, it matters little which. Likewise Joyce is God, Christ, Adam, the artist, the ancient kings of Ireland, the quintessential Irishman Parnell, the poet of *Chamber Music,* Stephen Hero, Stephen Dedalus, Richard Rowan, Leopold Bloom, Shem the Penman, and King Mark of Cornwall. Nora is Eve, the Virgin Mary, Emma Clery, E. C., the woman of *Chamber Music,* Bertha in *Exiles,* Ireland itself, Devorgil the Irish queen whose adultery brought the Saxons in, Kitty O'Shea, Molly Bloom, ALP, and Isolde. The conquerer is Satan, all of Nora Joyce's imagined lovers past and present, England and all it represents and all Englishmen, Robert Hand, Blazes Boylan, Shaun, Sir Tristram. (And all three figures can be recognized with a little effort in some of the stories of *Dubliners.*)

One further point. The personal myth, if the person is such as Joyce or Blake, shares the nature of those public myths, generated according to Jung in the collective unconscious and studied by folklorists and anthropologists, in that no two versions are quite the same. Incidents are displaced in sequence; personages may engross the available space or be attenuated to the vanishing point. Only a structuralist or deconstructionist approach can show that any two versions are really the same story. This is why Lenehan the betrayer is on the scene as a conventional character only some of the time. But his tracks are everywhere, though often very ghostly indeed; they are connected in every possible way, and they turn into one another as images do in dreams. They are often identifiable merely because they sound alike or because when visualized they look alike. Worst of all, when assembled out of context they appear to be an arbitrary collection (*bricolage?*) of heterogeneous trash.

The evidence may begin with Joyce himself, since Lenehan is a part of Joyce projected. We all know of his intensely dependent and ambivalent relationship with Nora, remarkably like Blake's, as Joyce evidently recognized, with Catherine Boucher, and of the imagined infidelities with which he obsessively tormented both of them. More closely to our theme, we know from many sources that Joyce considered that he had "created" Nora's soul, and that for him she represented Ireland (he calls her "my little strange-eyed Ireland!"). In 1903–4, when his family had reached its lowest ebb of sordid poverty, when he and his friends saw a real danger that he might degenerate into just another Dublin lounger and barfly, a "sporting vagrant" like Lenehan, and when he was saved by meeting Nora, he wore a white peaked cap and tennis shoes and carried the famous ashplant. He was photographed in this costume in front of a greenhouse (not the colloquial Dublin sense of the word), and when asked what he had been thinking at the time he neatly summed up that particular avatar of James Joyce by replying, "I was wondering would [C. P. Curran] lend me five shillings?" This raffish sponger and wastrel met Nora Barnacle and carried her over the sea in a creative betrayal of Ireland; and at first she thought, because of the cap, that he must be a sailor, and was attracted to him because he resembled her first love Sonny Bodkin. These ill-assorted data are the germs of a myth and the first building-blocks for Lenehan; the other gnomons are to be added later. But there is one important subtraction: the ashplant disappears. Why? Because it is a magic wand, an "augur's rod," because it is Siegfried's "Nothung," because it sustains a man and gives him strength and purpose.

This worthless "sailor" with cap and canvas shoes (who also, we should note, was a singer of no mean talents, sharing the platform with John McCormack shortly after he met Nora) is but dimly seen at first in Joyce's work. He may be hinted at in *Chamber Music* in the poem "Bright Cap and Streamers"; the speaker may be a woman, and may be following the singer while abandoning the "dreamer"; the title fits a sailor's cap. Yet "Lenehan" is clearly taking shape in the back of Joyce's mind, for in *Stephen Hero* a character called *Moy*nihan says that the *Decameron* "takes the biscuit" and affects French phrases, two of Lenehan's characteristic mannerisms, while we hear of the "cheap-looking white shoes" that Stephen wore. But the betrayer is not yet thoroughly detached from the hero who generates him, for in the *Portrait* Stephen wears "canvas shoes" as he picks up the magic ashplant and has the crucial vision of the wading girl, and on two occasions he eats "slim jim" out of a cricket cap.

With *Dubliners,* however, we arrive not only at the significant use of the word gnomon, but at a fully detached apprentice assistant betrayer, able to function on his own, if ineffectively. But first three of Lenehan's gnomons appear still in connection with the hero-narrator—those of music, gesture, and love—and so transformed by their context of ethereal pre-sexual adoration that the reader must take them upon trust, for nothing could seem more remote from sordid betrayal. The boy narrator of "Araby" (which we should note, however, is a story of youthful erotic idealism betrayed), swooning in "confused adoration" of Mangan's sister while he murmurs "*O love! O love!*" feels that "my body was like a harp and her words and gestures were like fingers running along the wires," and then perceives how the light "caught the white curve of her neck . . . and caught the white border of a petticoat." Surely, only excessive prurience could read anything more than remotely and chastely symbolic, or Tennysonian, sexual implications into that; but we shall see. And surely we do not expect to find Lenehan in "Eveline," but Hugh Kenner has pointed out that ships from the dock at Dublin's North Wall went to Liverpool, not Buenos Aires, so that Eveline, rather than losing her one chance of a good life in the New World, has drearily escaped betrayal and ruin in England, land of the conqueror (*The Pound Era*). Frank, who sings, and who wanted to take her away from Ireland and from the old father to whom she was a reluctant stay and support, is of course a sailor; Eveline remembers "the first time she had seen him . . . his peaked cap pushed back on his head." Her father had been quite right to say "I know these sailor chaps" and forbid her to see him.

Lenehan comes to full bloom in "Two Gallants." He also acquires his full complement of gnomons minus one or two, but some are attached to him, some merely in his vicinity, some overtly shown and some transformed. Joyce wrote "Two Gallants" ("And after all *Two Gallants*—with the Sunday crowds and the harp in Kildare street and Lenehan—is an Irish landscape" [*Letters of James Joyce*]) at a somewhat later stage in the development of his attitude toward symbol and image than the bulk of the *Dubliners* stories; it was his second favorite among them, and when his publisher wanted it dropped because of a few dangerous phrases Joyce indignantly protested that its removal would ruin the whole fabric of the book. The abundant critical work on "Two Gallants" has underlined the richness of its imagery of betrayal. All of its buildings, streets, and landmarks are associated with famous persons or incidents involved with the betrayal of Ireland in the eighteenth and nineteenth centuries; Lenehan is trapped, perhaps in Hell, for his wanderings take him in a circle; Corley represents the insolent English conqueror, Lenehan the Irish who abet the betrayal; the girl from whom Corley wheedles money is ruined Ireland; so is the symbolic harp played in the street; the gold piece Corley gets is associated with the feminine veiled moon that is constantly seen, while the lamps shine down like "pearls," which, we may remember for future reference, are the color of milk. Lenehan is called Corley's "disciple" (suggesting Judas); he follows him for any scraps that may fall. Like Frank's in "Eveline," "a yachting cap was shoved far back from his forehead," and he wears "white rubber shoes"; like Moynihan of *Stephen Hero* he says "that takes the biscuit" three times on three successive pages. He gazes at the moon and at the coin that resembles it. He peddles tips on horses, for "his name was vaguely associated with the racing tissues." Unlike Joyce he has reached the age of thirty without accomplishment but with "rotundity. . . . [H]is hair was scant and grey and his face . . . had a ravaged look." Like Joyce in 1904 he wishes that he could meet a girl who would save him through marriage, but, again unlike Joyce, he looks for purely financial salvation. Like him he is full of stories, limericks, riddles. He eats a plate of peas, and later we shall see why.

Two remoter gnomons may be noted for future reference. The servant girl who is Ireland has a white sailor hat and "fat red cheeks," details which are in no way out of the ordinary and would have no significance did not evidence arising years afterward indicate that they too are symbols of Ireland's betrayal in the Lenehan-archetype. But at the moment the traditional Irish harp of heraldry is more prominent, and is clearly more than a picturesque detail of setting, for Lenehan does a very odd thing. Obsessed with its music, some time after hearing it,

> His gaiety seemed to forsake him, and, as he came by the railings of the Duke's Lawn, he allowed his hand to run along them. The air which the harpist had played began to control his movements. His softly padded feet played the melody while his fingers swept a scale of variations along the railings after each group of notes.

The harpist's performance is described in unusual and rather strange detail.

> He plucked at the wires heedlessly, glancing quickly from time to time at the face of each new-comer and from time to

time, wearily also, at the sky. His harp too, heedless that her coverings had fallen about her knees, seemed weary alike of the eyes of strangers and of her master's hands. One hand played in the bass of the melody of *Silent, O Moyle,* while the other hand careered in the treble after each group of notes.

Aside from the repetition of the final phrases in the two passages, we note that as described the Irish harp might be a slave girl, stripped for exhibition on the block. The harpist manipulates her above and below, just as Lenehan does when imitating him, and in a concrete transformation of what the light did to Mangan's sister and what her voice and gestures did to the boy in "Araby." The song "Silent, O Moyle," bidding an Irish river be still, is from Thomas Moore's *Irish Melodies,* a lifelong companion of Joyce. It fits very well the theme of Irish betrayal, for it refers to the story of Fionnuala, daughter of the mythical king Lir, who has been turned into a swan and must fly over the earth for centuries until the coming of Christianity shall release her with the sound of the mass-bell. Not only Moore's words to this song, but to a number of others in his collection, repeat the theme of conquered Ireland as a disgraced and ruined maiden, waiting with forlorn hope for her deliverance.

After all this no one can doubt that Joyce associates Lenehan with betrayed Ireland, and on one level his message is obvious: as long as Ireland is full of Lenehans she will hope in vain for freedom and redemption. But Lenehan is not even the betrayer; why should Joyce take so much trouble to describe him in such loving detail, let alone make him play an imaginary harp and eat peas? The answer is found in Lenehan's further activities in *Ulysses* and *Finnegans Wake;* but only on the mythical level of action.

Though he has a fitful existence in half the episodes of *Ulysses,* and on both levels, he lives more importantly in the memories of Bloom and Molly, playing his mythical role, and sometimes only as a few scattered gnomons. On the literal level he still wears white shoes and a yachting cap; he proposes a riddle whose answer is "Rose of Castille," a clear reference to Molly, a rose from Gibraltar; he flirts with a barmaid at the Ormonde; and he betrays twice. The conqueror Corley has been replaced by conquering Blazes Boylan, who successfully seduces Irish Molly, and Lenehan betrays him by making him lose twenty pounds in betting on the wrong horse. The worthless tip, however, he got from someone named Stephen, who had steamed open a telegram from the racetrack, and he passed it on not only to Boylan but to Bantam Lyons, who through misunderstanding a remark of Bloom's was about to bet on the horse that eventually won. Thus in a typically devious Joycean way the assistant betrayer has been the means of avenging the husband on the seducer with the help of someone identifiable with the hero. But his traffic with "Stephen" has been indirect as well. We learn that after a quarrel he has discarded Corley, who has sunk into destitution and beggary; and in the "Eumaeus" chapter, Stephen Dedalus, now liberated and ready to assume the hero's role, does something totally unexpected: he performs the first act of charity that we have heard of from him. To Bloom's and Corley's astonishment he gives Corley, instead of the expected penny, half-a-crown, a coin which reflects the coin and the moon of "Two Gallants." Stephen symbolically completes the circle of Irish betrayal with an act of *agape* (even if the *agape* is partly the product of alcoholic relaxation) and so is able to escape from it. Twice in *Ulysses* Lenehan, with a "Stephen" to help, has been instrumental in breaking the circles he had helped to make. He has also broken free of the circle of realistic identity that trapped him in *Dubliners* and *Ulysses,* and is liberated to pursue disembodied adventures in the timeless cosmos of the *Wake*. But before following him there we must consider an adventure found in *Ulysses* only in memory.

Lenehan says in the "Wandering Rocks" episode that "there's a touch of the artist about old Bloom." The artist-as-hero or as God in Joyce always connives at his necessary betrayal-by-seduction, and so it is with Bloom. He remembers a dress Molly wore: significantly "She didn't like it," so that Bloom must have insisted on her wearing it; it "fitted her like a glove, shoulder and hips. Just beginning to plump it out well. . . . People looking after her." Molly, prominently displaying the charms above and below that the archetype demands, wore that dress at a public dinner ten years before, about a year after the end of normal sex between her and Bloom with the death of little Rudy, and must have been sexually aroused; for on getting home she told Bloom about her first kiss, received from Lieutenant Mulvey in Gibraltar (an echo of Nora Joyce's early beau *Willie* Mulvey), and when she fell asleep she gnashed her teeth. Bloom notes that the Lord Mayor had had his eye on Molly, perhaps thinking that she desired him. Bloom, however, does not know the truth; we do. First, the proofs of *Ulysses* reveal that Joyce originally intended to have Molly notice

Lenehan leering at her, not the Lord Mayor. Second, in "Penelope" Molly remembers that "Lenehan . . . was making free with me after the Glencree dinner." Lastly, in "Wandering Rocks" Lenehan tells in great detail just how he had made free with Molly, and his account is replete with his gnomons.

> Bloom and the wife were there. . . . Cold joints galore and mince pies. . . . Coming home it was a gorgeous winter's night. . . . Bloom and Chris Callinan were on one side of the car and I was with the wife on the other . . . a good load of Delahunt's port under her bellyband. . . . I had her bumping up against me. . . . She has a fine pair. . . . I was tucking the rug under her and settling her boa. . . . The lad stood to attention anyhow. . . . She's a gamey mare and no mistake. Bloom was pointing out all the stars . . . in the heavens. . . . I was lost, so to speak, in the milky way. . . . Lenehan . . . lifted his yachtingcap.

Here we have the sailor's cap, the stars and the moon, mince pies, a bellyband and a gamey mare, suggesting horses, manipulation of breasts and buttocks, and the Milky Way, repeating the pearly lights of "Two Gallants." Two points suggest themselves: the presence in, and extreme dispersal of this material through, *Ulysses* indicate both that to Joyce it is highly significant for the mythical life of all three actors, and that he went to a good deal of trouble to scatter it realistically among the confused fragments of the past. The episode is a transformation of the betrayal in "Two Gallants": the abstract harp has given way to a horsy lady of flesh, "little Ireland" like Nora Joyce, but horse-playing Lenehan is again the ineffectual seducer, and again he plays her bass and treble. And if this view of the episode as transformation seems too audacious, the following facts are pertinent. In "Nausicaa" Bloom, thinking of Molly's perfume luring a man she met at a dance, muses on "her high notes and her low notes"; at the end of "Oxen of the Sun" Lenehan, speaking of Molly, says that she has "a prime pair of mincepies . . . her take me to rests and her anker of rum"—Cockney rhyming slang for eyes, breasts, and bum; in the schema of symbols for *Ulysses* that Joyce sent his friend Carlo Linati, the last two episodes are called *stellare lattea* or Milky Way, and the symbol for Molly is the figure 8 lying on its side, which to mathematicians represents infinity but to Italians in jocose vulgarity a woman's breasts or buttocks. Lenehan's gnomons are all here. His eternal action is the same, but the

temporal clues to it have hitherto remained in Joyce's artful concealment, eternity in a grain of Blakean–Joycean sand.

With *Finnegans Wake* the difficulties of decoding increase many-
fold, and a thorough exploration is a daunting prospect; but even a few
short excursions can bring interesting results. Molly is sweet enough
to eat if she has mincepies attached to her, and one suspects that
"Lenehan" can be described through the linguistic mists when Shaun
or Jaun, always a hypocritical betrayer, says in his sermon to the
rainbow girls that he will, "replacing mig wandering handsup in
yawers so yeager for mitch, positively cover the two pure chicks of
your comely plumpchake with zuccherikissings." "Plumpchakes" are
plum cakes, not unlike the mincepies of Molly, but they are also
plump cheeks pronounced with an Irish brogue, and thus are the fat
cheeks of the slavey in "Two Gallants," with sugar kisses thrown in.

Joyce wrote the "Tristan and Isolde" and "Mamalujo" episodes of
the *Wake* rather soon after finishing *Ulysses*. The Irish queen, to be
married against her liking to a British father-figure and thus betray
Ireland, is loved beforehand by the morose but honorable Tristan,
therefore equating with Gretta Conroy in "The Dead" and Nora
Joyce, both of whom were loved by phthisic youths before meeting
their husbands. Well primed with *Ulysses* material, Joyce laid these
episodes aside until 1938, when they were amalgamated and linguistically enriched, the final version containing these (widely separated)
passages:

> Moykle ahoykling! . . . he was kiddling and cuddling and
> bunnyhugging scrumptious his colleen bawn . . . with his
> sinister dexterity, light and rufthandling, vicemversem her
> ragbags et assaucetiams, fore and aft. . . . after an oyster
> supper in Cullen's barn . . . the four of them, in the fair fine
> night, whilst the stars shine bright, by she light of he moon,
> we longed to be spoon. . . . (hear, Oh hear, Caller Errin!). . . .
> a strapping modern old ancient Irish prisscess, so and so
> hands high, such and such paddock weight . . . nothing
> under her hat but red hair and solid ivory. . . . (murky
> whey, asbtrew adim!)

Impenetrable or not, the text, like Lenehan's ride with Molly, includes
an aphrodisiac supper, four persons like the quartet on the jaunting car,
and the light of the moon and stars. But its earliest version readily
effects the decoding.

> As slow their ship . . . that handsome brineburnt six-footer
> Gaelic rugger and soccer champion . . . alternately rightleft-
> handled, fore and aft, on and offside, her palpable rugby and
> association bulbs . . . his useful arm getting busy on the
> touchline due south of her western shoulder. . . . pearlwhite
> passion-panting intuitions. . . . Hear, Oh hear, all ye caller
> herring! Silent be, O Moyle! Milky Way, strew dim light!
> . . . a strapping young modern and ancient Irish princess, a
> good eighteen hands high and scaling nine stone twelve
> paddock weight . . . [what do you suppose she cared] about
> tiresome old king Mark . . . ? Not as much as a pinch of
> henshit.

Tristan has become an Irish sailor (and football player), the Milky Way
and "Silent, O Moyle" are involved, and Isolde has become as horsy as
Molly, and as ready for adultery or at least manipulation by "Lenehan"
the horseplayer. The addition of rugger and soccer arises at least in part
from a Joycean transformation which scholarship has unraveled.

> Here the Freudian theory of games is in control of Joyce's
> metaphors as the Association footballs, which are spherical,
> sublimate for Iseult's breasts, while the Rugby footballs,
> which are oval, do the same for her buttocks. . . . [T]he ball
> used in English Rugby football is, though larger, of a much
> more gently rounded oval shape than that used in American
> football.

If the music has become partly Wagnerian, Lenehan is still harping on
breasts and buttocks by the silent Moyle in his eternal act of incomplete betrayal: "History as her is harped."

The "caller herring" force one out on a speculative limb. Herring
are found in many disguises in the *Wake,* including an Irish ballad,
"Herring the King"; and of course "herring" sounds like "Erin" and
"erring"—Ireland falling into error or sin, so that we find wordplay on
Ireland-Irrland-Erin-erring-herring-Heering-hearing. I propose that in
Joyce's symbolic system herring regularly stand for adultery or infidelity: first because of the wordplay just mentioned, second, because they
are notoriously prolific, and third because in the *Wake* they usually
appear in a context of sexual promiscuity. But they also appear elsewhere in the Joyce canon. "Caller" herring, the *OED* informs us, are
fresh herring (the word rhymes with *pallor*), and these figure in the play

Exiles. Robert Hand, who in that play may or may not have seduced Bertha (with her husband's connivance), thinks that Bertha is like the moon, and Joyce's notes for the play refer to the wicked queen whose adultery opened Ireland to the Saxons. In the third act, when Richard is convinced that Robert has seduced Bertha and Robert is about to protest that he has not, leaving Richard with "a wound of doubt" that will never heal, a fishwife is heard crying twice from offstage, "Fresh herrings! Fresh Dublin Bay herrings!" This is the only voice from the outside world in the play, and seems so arbitrary that it must be symbolically intended. Perhaps it relates to an incident in Joyce's life that has not transpired; but even in *Exiles* a gnomon of the Lenehan-archetype is present, seen by Joyce as essential, however seemingly irrelevant, to an ambiguously motivated attempt to secure fulfillment through betrayal. Lenehan is always an onlooker of the central action; but he will not be given his herrings again until gnomons become more important than veristic bodies—in the *Wake*.

One question of *bricolage* remains—the plate of peas Lenehan eats in "Two Gallants," which has puzzled many readers. Perhaps to a turn-of-the-century Dubliner this austere diet would be entirely commonplace for a nearly penniless person, though Joyce characterizes "grocer's peas" as "the most Spartan food"; perhaps Lenehan merely cannot afford some of the ham or the pudding also available. But the gnomon-hunter may turn to two bits of Joycean data for explanation. Erring Ireland is evidently a contemptible green *pea* for Joyce: his avatar Shem "would far sooner muddle through the hash of lentils in Europe than meddle with Irrland's split little pea." And a personage very like Lenehan in gnomons includes peas among them. Mr. Hurr Hansen (a Danish invader and a "steerner among *stars*") "hopes to fall in among a merryfoule of maidens *happynghome from the dance* . . . with their *peeas and oats upon a trencher* and the *toyms he'd lust in Wooming*. . . . Here's heering you" (italics mine). In Thomas Moore's *Irish Melodies* (Joyce's constant companion, as we have seen, and the source of "Silent, O Moyle") is a song called "The Time I've Lost in Wooing." Its words, though in Moore's prettified romantic vein, exactly echo Joyce's portrait in "Two Gallants" of the played-out, hopeless Lenehan and his incompetence with the fair sex. And the traditional tune to which the words are set is called "Peas upon a Trencher."

What has Lenehan, in sum, to tell us about Joyce's mind and art? We know that Joyce composed his art out of his life; but he also composed his life to a great extent, once he had got free of Dublin. If he felt that he had "created" Nora's soul as an essential part of his life, another equally essential part seems to have been a perpetual, self-created "wound of doubt" concerning betrayal. So far as we know, Nora, though sorely tried, was the essence of fidelity. She once contemplated leaving Joyce, but for the rest of their lives he had to manufacture the possibility of unfaithfulness. Since the factual basis was nil the infidelity had to be ambiguous, but this was an advantage, for we can torment ourselves much more effectively and elaborately with what we suspect than with what we know, as Othello discovered. In Joyce's myth of himself tentative or pseudo-betrayal had likewise to figure, as well as the genuine article. But as with his own epiphanies and Eliot's more famous objective correlative, in which named objects constitute the "formula of an emotion," that part of the equation could exist not only if embodied in a character, or in different characters in different works, but could be potent if merely evoked by the objects or gestures which identified, evoked, or defined those characters—their gnomons.

A revealing parallel is found in the strings of images which Joyce jotted down to identify, or rather to constitute, to *be,* as he composed, characters in *Exiles.* To us extremely arbitrary, they clearly meant much to Joyce, and like Lenehan they lead us to the central problem posed by the epiphany or objective correlative. Often largely by accidental association, the images mean everything to the artist; but he can only hope that he will be lucky and that they will have a like powerful effect, say the very same thing, to the reader. For Joyce "Lenehan" is the formula of pseudo-betrayal with sexual overtones (the sex act is never completed by him), sometimes as what we conventionally call a character, but always as a fixed store of objects and gestures in the mythmaking unconscious, to be called on when needed. But where Lenehan came from in the first place, and to what extent his gnomons transmit power and make sense, must be answered by the temperament of each individual reader.

A Blakean-structuralist view of the later Joyce is not entirely innovative. Recent writing on the *Wake* has argued that not only is it a "story about the Earwickers–Porters as a family of actors or archetypes," but that they are best seen as "fluid composites, involving an unconfined blur of historical, mythical, and fictitious characters, as well as non-human elements." The *sigla* Joyce used in his notes to control their flow are "like the table of chemical elements, . . . seldom found in nature in their pure form, and which compound with each other

. . . to constitute the natural world as we observe it." "Joyce in his ultimate work did not think in terms of fixed, named characters at all. Rather, he thought in terms of concepts, of characters which defy particularity." But the shapeless cloud of things and movements that condenses when it gets to the middle-period fictions to form Lenehan equally defies particularity, and tells us that throughout his *oeuvre* Joyce transcended the limiting concept of character as mere portraiture of putatively real people in a fixed place and time. Indeed, Joyce himself gave a timely announcement that this was his method, through the mouth of that perceptive young critic Stephen Dedalus:

> As we . . . weave and unweave our bodies . . . their molecules shuttled to and fro, so does the artist weave and unweave his image. And as the mole on my right breast is where it was when I was born . . . that which I was is that which I am and that which in possibility I may come to be.

Pure elements are composed of atoms, the specific element being constituted by their number and arrangement. If in the latter days of the Joycean cosmos the elements never exist in a pure state, their atoms are primordial and eternal. Lenehan reveals this fact in his subtext of recurring gnomons, unseen because lost among the myriad swirling verbal data of the universal text. The extension of this principle to other characters and to other authors tempts us with fascinating possibilities.

What Is a Woman . . . a Symbol Of?

Tilly Eggers

At the turning point in "The Dead," when the story shifts from a social situation to a personal experience, Gabriel asks himself, "What is a woman standing on the stairs in the shadow, listening to distant music, a symbol of?" Many critics interpret the question as further evidence of Gabriel's isolation, for he not only perceives his wife Gretta as "a woman" but also regards "a woman" as a symbol; others consider the question an insight into Joyce's conception of art. But no readers have met the challenge to answer the question directly, despite the surrounding clues of color, clothing, and attitude used throughout *Dubliners* and "The Dead" to associate particular women with the Blessed Virgin. The substance of the question—the relationship between a woman and an image of woman—has been ignored, even though the story is structured on a series of challenges by individual women to Gabriel's conventional perceptions of women, and even though Joyce himself was preoccupied with this subject throughout his life.

A major, although external, obstacle to the study of women in "The Dead" is the generally accepted opinion of Joyce's view of women which William T. Noon stated in his 1964 review of Richard Ellmann's biography: "There is in Ellmann's own book much Joycean personal evidence which, it seems, would oblige most readers, especially, one imagines, women readers, to conclude that Joyce was

From *James Joyce Quarterly* 18, no. 4 (Summer 1981). © 1981 by the University of Tulsa.

uncompromisingly an anti-feminist." The primary evidence, found in private and literary writings, is Joyce's use of extreme images of women, as virgins or whores or both, images interpreted as means to avoid recognizing women as individuals, either by elevating or by denigrating them. Because both Joyce and Gabriel perceive women in extremes as either spiritual or sensual and because of the autobiographical nature of the story, critics tend to identify the author exclusively with this male character and to equate their attitudes towards women, disregarding the broader perspective Joyce gives on Gabriel by the story as a whole and particularly by the figure of Gretta. I would not try to defend Joyce as a feminist, but I believe the categorical charge of anti-feminism directed at Joyce and the easy identification of him with Gabriel have ironically provided the excuse to simplify if not overlook the women in "The Dead." Reconsideration of virgin imagery in the story may help restore these women, and perhaps others in his works, to the place even Joyce grants them in fiction, and it may free readers, female and male, from an obligation which only prevents understanding of his vision of women.

Joyce's annunication in "The Dead," translated through the figures of Gretta and Gabriel, is that the virgin image does indeed have life. Out of the context of the preceding stories, in which he has shown the image isolating women from themselves and from men by its denial of individuality and sexuality, Joyce adapts the traditional image for perceiving women to his personal view, in a movement paralleling that of the story, from public, to personal, to the merging of personal and public. The closing image of Gretta and Gabriel lying together in bed, yet apart, recalls the image of them together in the shadows, yet separated from each other by the stairway; but Joyce makes the reader see differently what has been seen before because Gretta has increasingly qualified Gabriel's perspective and distanced the reader from him. Paradoxically, in the telling of her former lover, Gretta attains the figurative virginity Gabriel first announces on the stairway. Her individuality, which she affirms through her memories of girlhood, makes her inviolable, forever virgin; Gabriel cannot possess or destroy her, nor she him, and therefore the potential exists for them to extend themselves to each other.

Joyce's understanding of "virginity" as spiritual as well as physical is neither idiosyncratic nor peculiar in his works to this story. In Catholic theology, the Blessed Virgin is the Holy Mother, a paradox which Joyce seems to have found both practical, in allowing all women to be identified with her whatever their present roles or physical states, and philosophically accurate, in acknowledging the reality of the spiritual and the fluidity of time and identity. Although an examination of Joyce's use of virgin imagery in earlier or later works is not within the scope of this paper, nowhere does he restrict the imagery to women who are physically virgin: throughout he implies that "The soul like the body may have a virginity."

A widely accepted critical view attributes to Joyce a triadic categorization of Woman as Virgin-Mother-Temptress, but too often the multiple image is understood as static—slots to contain characters by either realistic or ironic definition, not as dynamic—useful precisely because it can never quite fit an individual, all at once, at one time. As with the Bloom-Ulysses parallel, the juxtaposition of the virgin image with other perspectives on a particular woman is not simply true or untrue, elevating or denigrating. Instead, as Wolfgang Iser argues about the mythic parallel, the various, conflicting "schematized views" define the "gaps" (or form the "parallax" to use Joyce's own term), rather than define the character. These "indeterminacies" evoke the aesthetic response, the involvement of the reader in the creation of the text. Joyce associates Gretta with the Virgin to express what Gretta is by saying what she is not any longer, and to say what she was and therefore what she still is and will be. At the same time the image distances the character, as do all views but especially those which call attention to themselves as views, while it identifies her with other female characters, in this story and beyond. But as the distance between Gretta and Gabriel makes communication between them possible, so the distance between the character and the reader, the identification of Gretta with all women, and the discrepancies between the various internal perspectives, all force the reader to formulate yet another image of her, having learned that no one image captures her reality completely. Gretta exists beyond the perspectives on her, but through the creative process of reading the reader participates in her reality.

The ambiguity of the virgin image in "The Dead," as of the story as a whole, reflects not only Joyce's ambivalent feelings after two years of exile from Ireland but also his understanding that in the incompleteness of art exists its potential. Darcy O'Brien, in the most extensive study of Joyce's attitude towards women and the Virgin ideal, argues that the artist never freed himself from the cult of the virginal. I believe O'Brien accurately describes the younger writer of *Chamber Music* and *Stephen Hero* and the young artist, Stephen, but that he fails to recognize the mature artist of "The Dead," who did not free himself from the virgin image but forged it for his own use. How Joyce adapts this traditional image provides a model for how the mature artist adapts the other forms of Ireland.

"The Dead," like the first story in *Dubliners,* is about the relationship between form and meaning, flesh and spirit, but in "The Sisters" Joyce implies the elements are irrevocably asunder, while in the final story he first explores the ambiguity of many forms and thereby prepares the reader for the development in the second part of the possibilities in one form, the virgin image. He focuses on Gabriel's confusions about his identity, his perceptions, and his actions at the party, itself a formality which though predictable and traditional provides the context for the character's views on languages, literature, art, religion, history, and music to be shaken. But the threat extending throughout the story, after the scene changes from the dance to the hotel, is to Gabriel's perceptions of woman. Although he perceives only his wife, and her indirectly, as a Virgin-figure, his confrontations with the apparently more virginal women—Lily, Miss Ivors, and the spinster relatives—evoke details and issues associated traditionally and in the preceding stories with this ideal of womanhood. As the story progresses, the conflict between Gabriel's expectations and what individual women declare themselves to be becomes the metaphor incorporating all other relationships between perception and reality.

The opening sentence in the story—"Lily, the caretaker's daughter, was literally run off her feet"—defines the character in terms of her father and of her role as a servant. The hyperbole, by calling attention to itself, underscores the routine, mechanical activity of the figure as it warns the reader to question the literal meanings of the words that follow, to read beyond the stated to the unstated and to look past the stereotype to the person. Most obviously, Gabriel's statement in the form of a question reveals his inability to respond to the individual because he assumes Lily is a typical, young, unmarried, female servant—"I suppose we'll be going to your wedding one of these fine days with your young man, eh?" In this way Lily does serve to characterize Gabriel as a person whose perceptions, like his scintillating glasses, screen rather than clarify his vision of external reality, but she is also someone asking for respect from him, from "The men that is now," and from the reader.

Crediting her, the reader realizes that she is like Gabriel, formal and rote, when she asks, when there is snow on his overcoat, "Is it snowing again, Mr. Conroy?" Her question has never been understood as an indication of her condescension and isolation, as has his, but it should not be overlooked. Lily's politeness interprets Gabriel's formality while it reveals her as one other character confused about who she is and what she does. Their idle chatter, their "palaver," like most of the talk during the evening has the potential for hiding or disclosing character and for making or prohibiting contact. Gabriel's "wrong tone" is not as he thinks the only reason for her anger, and his question about maturity and marriage is as appropriate as it is disrespectful. Aunt Kate offers a broader, more understanding explanation for Lily's response—"She's not the girl she was at all." The girl wants recognition as a mature person by Gabriel and as more than a sexual object by all men—"what they can get out of you." Lily, whose name is that of the flower traditionally associated with the Blessed Virgin, is a "slim, growing girl" who is developing from the child with the rag doll, whom Gabriel remembers, into a sensuous woman, to whom Gabriel has difficulty adjusting. Her identity is not fixed, and like Gabriel, who recalls his youth and anticipates aging throughout the evening, Lily cannot yet accept her changing identity. Except for one of her "back answers," Lily acts as a submissive handmaid, but the complexities of her assertion are necessary to her characterization and those of Gabriel and the other women, especially Gretta.

The brief episode with Lily provides the first step towards the conclusion when Gabriel realizes that Gretta is someone other than his wife, a person apart from the role she performs in relation to him. His question to Lily anticipates his question about Gretta on the stairway, even though here he assumes the role is the person and later he puzzles over the relationships between roles, multiple identities, and the individual. Also, by revealing the limitations of Gabriel's perceptions, the question to Lily conditions the reader to make independent interpretations. The conclusion, in retrospect, recasts the incident so that Lily's self-assertion is as significant as Gabriel's response to it. She, like Gretta, demands that he recognize the girl she was as the woman she is, and vice versa. Unlike Gretta, however, Lily cannot understand herself as at once child, daughter, servant, girl, and woman, accepting the continuity of change within herself, and therefore her various roles threaten rather than strengthen her sense of self.

In contrast, the technical presentation of Lily reflects the very understanding she lacks. Joyce uses the roles and associations with the

Virgin ideal to present Lily, and then he uses the conflicts she and Gabriel have with the ill-fitting form to indicate the ambiguous individual which neither she nor Gabriel can comprehend. Joyce continues to demonstrate that it is the distance between the traditional form for perceiving woman and the distinctive traits presented which gives room for the individual to emerge.

Molly Ivors also challenges Gabriel's perceptions of woman by not behaving in the manner he expects of a female, friend, colleague, and dance partner. She and Gabriel are particularly threatening to each other because they are similar in asserting their superiority to common humanity but different in their modes of assertion. Gabriel isolates himself through observing social formalities, while Miss Ivors removes herself by rejecting them; the dangers and possibilities inherent in social forms become clearer to the reader by their interaction. As with Lily, Gabriel's encounter with Molly most obviously serves to show his vulnerability, the fraudulent exterior which belies insecurity, but his comments about her, as they reflect negatively on him, do give valid insight into her. Molly Ivors is distinctive among the guests because she is young, energetic, and intelligent; but, despite the positive aspects of this view of woman, it simplifies the complex character Joyce presents.

Gabriel questions the relationship between Molly's public actions and her personal identity—"Had she really any life of her own behind all her propagandism?" Molly does seem unable to integrate her contradictory feelings for Gabriel, accusing him one moment of insincerity and then reassuring herself and him the next by grasping his hand warmly, as if she thinks she cannot be both friend and critic at once. She leaves the party abruptly before dinner because she does not "feel in the least hungry"—perhaps a logical reason but an insufficient one. Her other excuse for leaving is that she has "already overstayed her time." Alongside the ancient aunts, her sense of time seems foolish; the young woman can learn from the elderly ladies who know that time is not theirs and that it will continue after they die.

Gabriel's thought, "there was a time for all things," also qualifies Miss Ivors's attitude about time, and together their ideas foreshadow the understanding of time and identity expressed in the conclusion of the story. "The Dead" is built structurally and thematically upon the conception of time which minimizes the importance of each moment, as being only part of a whole, as it makes each moment vital, as a separate entity. The biblical allusion implies forms broader than social manners, but Gabriel's sense of propriety does lead him to a wisdom beyond his present understanding, while Molly's rejection of social graces separates her from both the life and death of the dance. She will not submit to time. She wants to turn back time and recapture Irish culture and language, because she cannot yet accept that the past exists within her and that her language is the language of her ancestors. Like Lily and Gabriel, she will not submit to an identity larger than herself, one encompassing other women or all humanity, because she feels it will deny not develop who she is. Gabriel's description of her recalls Aunt Kate's remark about Lily—"Of course the girl or woman, or whatever she was, was an enthusiast." Neither young woman can yet integrate her multiple selves into a person whose spirit and actions are mutually reinforcing.

Gabriel patronizingly offers to accompany Molly home, as he later imaginatively protects Gretta as they walk to the hotel, but Gretta places his politeness and Molly's reply, "I'm quite well able to take care of myself," in a broader context when she calls her "the comical girl." Later in the hotel room, as Gretta seeks Gabriel's comfort without fear of threat to her personal identity, she again qualifies Molly's assertion of independence. The conclusion develops further the problems between Molly and Gabriel about the relationships between growth and stability, assertion and submission, self and others.

Joyce's characterization of Miss Ivors anticipates the conclusion and suggests that although he has not settled such differences, he has discovered how to employ them. Molly is distinctive among the characters for the very reason that she is one in a network of cross-identifications and common concerns which continue to build as the story progresses. As the dance accommodates both her charges and her warm grasps into patterns of ritualized motion, Joyce incorporates individuals into an overall pattern with universal meaning, without subordinating anyone to the design. He indicates the uniqueness of Molly Ivors by showing what she has in common with the society she rejects and with the ideas Gabriel represents that she attacks. Joyce arranges opposing elements to reveal the character who defies such polarization.

The Misses Morkans unintentionally threaten Gabriel with their energy and openness. He thinks near the end of the story that he is a "pennyboy" for silly women, one who plays runs without melody, one who sings "Arrayed for the Bridal," all who are "toddling round" serving people who laugh at them. But that is not the only way to see them, or him. Gabriel is solicitous and sincere, generous and selfish, and the three women are as wise as they are ignorant, as alive as they are dead. It is to Gabriel's credit that he attends to them and evidence of his limitations when he denies their value.

The reader who attends to them grows aware of the delicate reciprocity in each between a personal sense of self and a public sense of self defined by their relationships with each other, with their extended family, with their students and friends, and with the past, present, and future. In contrast to the younger women, Lily and Molly, they assert themselves through conventional forms of music, conversation, and hospitality. They give themselves without fear of loss, though loss of self in death is certainly near for the aunts. They kiss Gabriel "frankly," their positions in life are "self-won," and they "turned crimson with pleasure." Aunt Kate almost doubles herself laughing at a joke she is not sure she understands, and she fiercely defends her sister and the rights of women against the pope and the "honour of God." Mary Jane's hands lift from the keyboard like those of a "priestess in momentary imprecation" as Aunt Kate stands nearby to aid her; but the niece is also the "main prop of the household" now, and despite their ages the aunts do their share. The women provide for themselves, as they accept a higher providence. The tone of Gabriel's speech about the tradition of genuine hospitality may be questionable, but Aunt Kate's comment about the pope's injustice in turning women out of the choirs is passionate and convincing—"But there's such a thing as common everyday politeness and gratitude." She believes that social formalities can direct and express human feelings and actions. Because the women respect conventions, they can turn them to their own purposes. Although their community is limited, the spinsters contribute to cyclical regeneration by infusing the past into the present, by transmitting music, conversation, and food into youth. Gabriel's allusion to the Graces, three in one, is appropriate for their unity defines the uniqueness of each and their individuality creates their relationship. They give themselves to others and are rejuvenated.

Before the stairway scene, no one pays much attention to Gretta. The aunts kiss "Gabriel's wife" and regard her only as wife and mother. The narrator refers to her as "his wife." Her first name does not appear for several pages into the story, and then Aunt Kate only mentions her to identify the transmitter of information about Gabriel to Gabriel. But it is because of, not in spite of, such indirection that Gretta attains vitality and clarity even in the first part; and Joyce continues to use various methods which distance and yet paradoxically define the ambiguity, the changing reality, of character: light and mirror imagery, shifts between distant and close-up perspectives, juxtapositions of what Gretta says and does with what Gabriel says, does, and thinks, the song from the past, and the story-within-the-story. These are similar to the techniques Joyce uses with other women in "The Dead" and, perhaps less consciously and competently, with women throughout *Dubliners,* to assert the reality of the spirit, the multiplicity of identity, and the fluidity of time.

These attributes, symbolized by the Blessed Virgin and traditionally called "feminine," Joyce also associates with Gabriel through comparable devices: reflection imagery, such as lights, mirrors, and windows; wall pictures; fictionalizing of the past; the narrator's use of "as if" in interpreting Gabriel; and the internal perspective, which renders the discrepancy between internal and external, particularly between Gabriel's fantasies of Gretta and their present relationship. All of these devices provide multiple, conflicting perspectives on Gabriel, indicate his shifting levels of consciousness, and show his gaining new angles on himself. Gabriel can accept the fluidity in his own identity, letting past and future reinforce the present, although Joyce reveals different degrees in his acceptance. Because there is no single image to incorporate these attributes for man, as the virgin image does for woman, Joyce associates Gabriel with the Archangel by name, with the priesthood by Constantine and his home of Monkstown, and with Christ by his presiding over the last dinner. Each of these images represents spirituality, the universal in the particular, and passivity as a form of action.

The "feminine" qualities in Gabriel have been defined as his weaknesses, while the "masculine" aspects of the women—their assertiveness and independence—have been excused as problems of youth and age or praised as repudiations of conventional expectations. The independence of Gretta, who is a middle-aged wife and mother, cannot be dismissed so easily as a matter of age or regarded as a rejection of traditional images; nor can it be explained away as the result of something outside rather than inherent in her, the regrettable result of Gabriel's weaknesses as a man, his inability to satisfy her. But Joyce implies through the story-within-the-story, Gretta's girlhood experience with Michael, that Gretta is independent yet related in the present to Gabriel. Joyce seems to regard variations in sex roles and stereotypes not as problems but as essential and inevitable ingredients of a person. Gretta remains distant and distinct, assertive and submissive, the typical wife, mother, and woman and yet an individual: the dynamic relationships between what are defined as irreconcilable opposites seem to be a primary concern and method of Joyce's characterization. Because in the figure of Gretta he achieves a working harmony of contradictions, she is central to a study of Joyce's attitude towards women, towards the relationship between female and male, and towards the capacities of language and traditional forms of perceptions to express his vision.

Although others define Gretta as "Gabriel's wife," neither her relationship to him nor her identity is fixed by that role. She possesses a flexibility in the roles she plays and an ease with the ambiguity of her identity which the younger women and Gabriel lack. She stands by his side to sympathize with his discomfort about Miss Ivors, but she aligns herself with Molly and "her people" of Connacht against Gabriel when he refuses to visit the west of Ireland. She breaks out "into a peal of laughter" and teases Gabriel about galoshes while expressing resistance to him—"To-night even he wanted me to put them on, but I wouldn't." Gretta would walk freely into the snow, but she will also protect herself from the snow; her position in the story is somewhere between Michael, whose selflessness leads him into the rain to death, and Gabriel, whose self-possession protects him from the snow and from life. Gretta gives herself in laughter and concern for others as she maintains an integrity of self apart from others. At first Gabriel feels proud of her, and his "admiring and happy eyes" wander "from her dress to her face and hair." When she asks for recognition of her identity apart from him rather than for admiration and consideration as his possession, he grows insecure. He cannot accept the fluidity in Gretta: in the stairway scene he gains perspective on her, seeing her not only as his wife but as a woman and a symbol. This distance is the grounds for his mounting emotions, which are intensified by fantasies of their courtship—the heliotrope envelope, the ticket placed in her warm palm, and their watching the man make bottles in the blazing furnace—and by his memories of their secret life together which burst like "tender fires of stars." Although he becomes abstracted from the present, he trembles with annoyance at her abstraction and longs to be the "master of her strange mood." But he cannot, for she is not wholly present nor his. He cannot understand her independence as reinforcing their future, although his own life is one of abstraction, self-reflection, and various experience through art, memory, and imagination.

Progressively throughout the story, Gretta asserts herself while Gabriel loses confidence in himself: their movements in different directions interpret each other. As Joyce focuses on the interaction of the "feminine" and "masculine" in Gretta and Gabriel, he focuses on the interaction between them, forcing the reader to respond to the combination of male and female on the broader, structural level also.

The stairway scene is a turning point in the story, the pivot between the dance and the hotel. It is simultaneous with the cab scene which precedes it in the story's chronology, and this tuck in time sets the scene in relief. Joyce contrasts the slapstick, outdoor episode with the introspective, indoor scene, and he changes the focus from a close-up of many characters in conversation and action to a more distant perspective on a woman and a man, standing together in the shadows apart from all others, yet separated from each other within the shadows. Gabriel remains in the foreground, but his position rather than being superior to Gretta's is defined by hers. The glittering party light, which illuminated Gabriel's self-reflections, dims as he looks outward and directs attention to Gretta and their relationship. The independence which Gretta and other women assert at the party becomes a matter of technique as well as of theme.

On the stairway Gabriel perceives Gretta in outline form. He does not directly answer his question—"What is a woman standing on the stairs in the shadow, listening to distant music, a symbol of?"—but he notes the details, such as the woman's grace and mystery, the color blue of her hat, her elevated position, and her other-worldly attitude, which are traditional associations with the Blessed Virgin that Joyce employs throughout *Dubliners*. But while Gretta is a human symbol of the Virgin ideal, she is also a composite portrait of women in *Dubliners*, the symbol of all women. Like many characters in the collection, Gabriel identifies a woman with the Virgin, but unlike any of them he can perceive the woman as spiritually and physically desirable; what Gabriel cannot do is perceive her an integrated person, independent of himself. The peculiar phrasing of his question reflects his confusion about the relationship between the human and the symbolic, but it also reflects the reinterpretation of the virgin image which Joyce has been preparing the reader for and will continue to develop; there is a reciprocity between a woman's symbolic significance and her individual reality.

Despite the confusion about the relationship between the ideal and the human reflected in Gabriel's question, his perception of the woman as the Virgin excites rather than inhibits his sexual passion, but he responds to her in either one extreme or the other. A connection exists for him between the opposite perceptions, but not until later does he realize that neither definition of Gretta, as spiritual or sensual, captures the reality of Gretta. For the reader, the series of challenges by individual women to Gabriel's conventional perceptions has cumulatively called into question the reader's own image of woman being formulated in the process of reading. The reader has learned to expect fluidity and partiality in characterization, and so participation in the interaction of the opposite perceptions adequately approximates the ineffable reality of Gretta. The stairway becomes a metaphor for the distance which connects separate people—Gretta walks down the stairway to Gabriel who follows her up the stair to the hotel. Likewise, the fiction, which engages and distances the reader, allows for the ambiguity of reality.

The light upon Gretta begins to change after the stairway scene from shadow to "dusty fanlight," to a "dull yellow light," to "ghostly light," and out of the increasing darkness she gradually attains reality. In the hotel room, she walks in, out, and upon light, as though it were more tangible than she. The light questions both the substantiality of her physical form and the imperceptibility of her spirit. Gretta retains a transparency like that of a "shade," which can be seen through but which makes clear that which is inaccessible. She appears like a reflection, a shadow of herself, but the self is insubstantial and remote while the concrete form is present. Her body assumes shape in a mirror, but it is like a shell from which the spirit has been transported by song and memory. At the same time, details of her movements and Gabriel's sensitivity to her verify her present physical reality. Gretta dries her eyes "with the back of her hand like a child"; Gabriel caresses her hand which is "warm and moist" but unresponsive. The woman is a child: Gretta is absent and present, alive and dead. The figure of Gretta testifies to the paradoxical nature of reality suggested by the title and implied in the characterization of others.

Through her story about Michael Furey, through the mirror of fiction, Gretta becomes divided from herself and made whole. The telling actualizes her inner reality, as it verifies her external reality. It affirms her existence in the past as it makes the past present; through memory and fiction she revives her younger self which confirms her mature self. Her identity apart from Gabriel provides a context for, without denying, her identity as lover, wife, and mother. In the telling of her story, she freely gives herself to Gabriel, but the revelation of her girlhood on Nun's Island establishes the distance between them by forcing him to see the girl he never knew. The distance between them and the reader is also a story, a mirror which is true as it indicates further truth.

Gabriel acts as interpreter of Gretta and her story, but what she expresses through her own actions, words, and silences contradicts his understanding. Therefore, the reader is forced to stand back from Gretta and Gabriel and view the fiction as a whole. Gabriel cannot accept truth in both the woman and the girl, in the teller and the tale, and believes one falsifies the other. Watching Gretta sleep, Gabriel thinks she is dead to him, that her life as a girl denies her life with him—"He watched her while she slept as though he and she had never lived together as man and wife." He cannot credit both the shadow and the substance, what she is independent of him and what she is with him; he does not understand the reciprocity between contradictory elements.

Gabriel also questions the completeness of Gretta's story—"Perhaps she had not told him all the story." By this point, the reader understands that completeness applies to reality, not art; Gretta's story, Gabriel's interpretation, Joyce's story, the reader's interpretation are all incomplete, but not invalid. Gretta does not express herself completely in the account or in the act of telling; the expression of self paradoxically reinforces her separate identity. What Gretta was and what she is at the moment indicate that there is still more to the reality of Gretta: she is a character in the process of becoming. Gabriel does not believe in the reality of ghost stories and regards the past as sad memories to brood upon; he believes that the spirit of Michael holds Gretta in the past and that she has "locked in her heart for so many years that image of her lover's eyes." However, Gretta's story has revived Michael, and his image is part of her always. She is "perished alive" within herself, as Kate and Julia remark, but she rekindles her past to renew her future. The girl in her gives life to the woman, and she falls asleep, like a child and old woman, confident that sleep prepares her for waking. Gabriel observes that her "girlish beauty" has faded and that her face is no longer the face Michael loved, but through her story Gretta verifies that she still is the girl Michael died for and that her past is present within her. The hair on the pillow is the hair of the wife drying her hair a few days before, of the Virgin figure on the stairway, and of the sensual woman: Gretta is continuous and changing.

As Gabriel unconsciously shifts from the reality of the "petticoat string" to the reality of "the shade of Patrick Morkan and his horse," the reader shifts from the literal truth Gabriel perceives at the moment to the truth visible from a more distant perspective. Gabriel recalls his speech, the Misses Morkans, the assertions of immortality, all as foolish, but the ambiguity of what has occurred qualifies his judgment. It is true that Gabriel has never "felt like that himself towards any woman": he has not died for someone. It is true that "such a feeling must be love," but it is also true that Gabriel's feelings for Gretta are love. Gabriel will not die like Michael Furey, but neither will he "fade and wither dismally." Gabriel will continue living, a journey which moves westward and eastward, between past and present, between life and death. Gabriel perceives himself and Gretta becoming shades like Michael, and he interprets the progress towards transparency and death as movement towards unreality. However, Michael's love became real through his death, and he became immortal through memory and fiction. As Gabriel feels his identity slipping from him, he becomes more complex and human, and as Gretta asserts her individuality, she also becomes more ambiguous and real. The reader plays the various perspectives off against each other.

The "few light taps upon the pane" direct Gabriel's attention from his individual dissolution to the fluidity common to the universe, and they once again draw the reader's attention away from Gabriel, to Gretta and Gabriel, to all humanity. The dramatic nature of the final scene objectifies and qualifies Gabriel's perceptions. In losing himself, he may find himself and be reborn. Life and death are functions of each other and thereby exist within each other. The gate which separates the living from the dead also connects them. Christ represents God to man; He is and is not God. Snow, an ambiguous white image, covers and connects as it distinguishes the individual forms of Ireland.

The final image in "The Dead" is not Gabriel's dream vision but the reader's image of a woman and man falling asleep, together in bed yet separate from each other. The image recalls the similar relationship between the two when they are together in the shadows apart from all others, yet separated by the stairway. But by the close of the story, Joyce has carefully qualified Gabriel's perspective and distanced the reader by the series of encounters with women, especially with Gretta, who is the culmination of the independent spirits of the women who came before her. The image is ambiguous: the people are separate and together, present and absent, on the border between consciousness and unconsciousness. The man interprets his loss of identity as death and distance between himself and the woman as denial of their relationship. His feelings may be jealousy that someone knew her first and regret that she is not "his" to be proud of; but, despite her thoughtful mood, neither in the telling nor in her gently falling asleep does Gretta express resentment or disappointment toward either Gabriel or Michael because of a loss she suffers. Instead, her past and Michael Furey are alive in her. The woman implies that memory of her "girlself" renews her woman self and that expression of independence affirms a connection. The ambiguity resulting from this juxtaposition of viewpoints is specified further by the earlier image of the woman and man on the stairway. In the end, Gretta remains isolated, virgin to Gabriel. He understands her spiritually and sensually, but, while these aspects reveal her, they also reveal a reality somewhere beyond. Joyce shows that the possibility of a love relationship depends on separation, not on possession or subordination of one to another. As in the original Annunciation, the characters in this drama have only limited understanding of their roles, yet they assume symbolic dimensions.

Joyce does, then, use the virgin image to avoid direct presentation of a woman, but his indirection is recognition of the reality which cannot be made present wholly in art. Characterization becomes a quest for that which achieved would be its own dialectical negation. With a holistic conception of reality and a consequent acceptance of the limitations of language, Joyce indicates individuality, presence, and completeness by expressing commonality, absence, and partiality; one term calls forth its opposite, for their meanings are interdependent, but the reality which is both at once is beyond either. More specifically, "virginity" and "non-virginity" define each other, but neither defines the self who is both at once, if by potential alone, and much else. The reader responds to the interplay between the mutually defining terms and thereby participates in the motion of reality.

The technical presentation of Gretta reveals her to the reader as it reveals the limitations of the fictional perspective on her. The indirect focus, Gabriel's limited understanding, and her own statements, all indicate her more distant reality. Problems of identity surround all the characters in *Dubliners,* whom Joyce presents through their relationships with others, through circumstances, and through sexual, social, economic, political, and religious roles and expectations, all of which tend to subsume the characters rather than define them as individuals. But in "The Dead" the problems become the means for creating characters in the ambiguity of humanity. Joyce uses what is typical about Gretta to show what is unique. He relies on the reader's need to make sense of multiple, sometimes conflicting, viewpoints. What Gabriel gradually realizes about Gretta, the reader experiences through her; the reader perceives Gretta from external and internal perspectives without knowing her completely. She remains apart by an otherness which her spirituality and sensuality suggest. Joyce indicates the motion of reality through respect for the virginity, the integrity, of character.

Joyce's art is an act of re-creation. In "The Dead" Joyce reinterprets the virgin image as a form for indicating without fixing women. The image incorporates contradictions—the symbolic with the human, sexual purity with motherhood, isolation and other-worldliness with a common identity among all women, and passivity and activity. Therefore, Joyce can adapt the image to particular women, of different times, places, roles, and ages; he can use the static image to express the fluidity of time and identity and the individuality which defies classification. The word "virginity" assumes meaning as Joyce asserts the paradox that opposites are inherently related on the basis of their differences—"virginity" makes "unvirginity" possible, as the spiritual and physical define each other. He asserts that opposite perceptions are not the identity which is virgin and unvirgin at once but that they can paradoxically express fluidity and individuality by their fixity. Joyce's vision of woman neither denies the individual, as critics have thought, nor does it glorify the individual or the female, as some might wish. Through the reciprocity among these perceptions, Joyce's art achieves the vitality of life.

Structure and Meaning
in Joyce's "The Sisters"

Phillip Herring

In an important article on James Joyce's *Dubliners* story "The Sisters," Burton A. Waisbren and Florence L. Walzl argue convincingly that Father Flynn suffered from paresis, otherwise known as syphilis of the central nervous system, and that Joyce took some care to describe numerous symptoms of this disease while calling it simply, though ambiguously, *paralysis*. This explains much—why the priest is surrounded by an air of mystery that his young friend cannot comprehend, why he seems to have been "defrocked," why adults in the story are so uneasy about their friendship. By hinting at syphilis without using a more specific term, Joyce could shock readers, especially those attuned to the implications, while escaping censorship. Surely the "truth" about Father Flynn has been discovered.

Evidence to contradict the Waisbren-Walzl thesis is unlikely to surface, but it could be attacked on grounds of relevance. The story was carefully constructed so that the point is precisely that neither the boy nor the reader can know the truth they seek; that all appears inscrutable is hence a *donnée* of "The Sisters." How useful, then, is extratextual evidence such as Joyce's interest in syphilis (as seen in the *Letters*) and the fact that *paralysis* was a common euphemism for syphilis in Joyce's day? We begin with this example because at issue here is not merely how we interpret one short story, but rather whether or not it is possible to interpret Joyce at all with any degree of

From *The Seventh of Joyce,* edited by Bernard Benstock. © 1982 by Indiana University Press.

validity, for to illustrate the general ambiguity of Joycean texts is to effectively sabotage Joyce scholarship. What more could a scholar show us than how such a text arrived in its final, ambiguous form? This is the central issue in Joyce criticism today, and one that was hotly debated in recent symposia. On one side are the traditional scholars, who do research, study manuscripts, and cite evidence, and on the other side are practitioners of contemporary literary theory, who are skeptical about language and what it can do.

Although my own work has been "scholarly," and in my two books I have taken pains to show Joyce's debts to his predecessors and how, like a scholar, he did research on his subjects, in this paper I wish to show that Joyce intended to give aid and comfort to the enemy, that he generated structures and meanings in a precociously experimental way as early as the first story of *Dubliners*.

On numerous occasions Joyce provided guideposts to interpretation, but it has not been generally accepted that "The Sisters" itself functions in that capacity. Still, on one level, the story is about ambiguity, about the impossibility of reaching certainty. His seemingly contradictory strategy of producing both ambiguous texts and the keys to interpreting them may have had the effect of keeping the professors busy, one of Joyce's stated purposes, but it also shows his early skepticism about our ability to get at the truth except in fragments, to understand finally and completely the impressions that our senses bring us, to analyze and interpret experience with a high degree of certainty, and to express ourselves unambiguously in eel-slippery language.

The reader of "The Sisters" encounters several barriers to understanding: the text is full of elliptical language filtered through the consciousness of a bewildered youth who broods over the deceased Father Flynn and the meaning of their friendship. Readers are easily deceived into thinking that the boy is merely naïve, and that greater maturity would be an advantage to him in wrestling with the holes in meaning, an illusion that should be dispelled at the story's end, when we are denied access to the boy's final thoughts. His reaction to new and probably decisive information is cloaked in ellipses, while the reader is left to fill in the gaps. If the truth about Father Flynn has been left to the reader, can it not be said that this truth is of necessity relative?

The opening lines of the early version of the story, published in *The Irish Homestead* in 1904, illustrate that indeterminacy was no late addition (italics mine):

Three nights in succession I had found myself in Great Britain Street at the hour, as if by *providence*. Three nights I had raised my eyes to that lighted square of window and *speculated. I seemed to understand* that it would occur at night. But in spite of the providence which had led my feet and in spite of the reverent curiosity of my eyes *I had discovered nothing*.

This theme of uncertainty, reminiscent of Conrad's *Heart of Darkness*, was reinforced in the story's final version with the addition of three words widely accepted as keys to interpretation in *Dubliners* as well as "The Sisters." Here the boy's interpretative difficulty, first attributed to fickle Providence and human frailties, is now located in language itself: "Every night as I gazed up at the window I said softly to myself the word *paralysis*. It had always sounded strangely in my ears, like the word *gnomon* in the Euclid and the word *simony* in the Catechism." No logic binds these three italicized words together—only the strangeness of their sounds in the boy's ear. To him the meanings are private ones, perhaps only loosely connected, if at all, to dictionary definitions. The words seem to cast a spell over him and, at the same time, point to many interpretive possibilities about which the sensitive reader may speculate. Father Flynn was a paralytic; what do *gnomon* and *simony* have to do with him? Can these terms be applied to anyone or anything else? Yet the reader, like the boy, is impelled to seek a truth he can never find: the three words neither lead them toward illumination nor can they be dismissed as meaningless. This is the dilemma of following the lead of the author-critic-tease who provides keys to understanding an ambiguous text. My essay is about how it is possible to use one term—*gnomon*—as an instrument of interpretation within this curious epistemological framework.

Let us take a closer look at the key words. In *A Portrait* young Stephen Dedalus says, "Words which he did not understand he said over and over to himself till he had learned them by heart: and through them he had glimpses of the real world about him." The comprehension of key concepts is also the primary means of orientation for the boy in "The Sisters," who, with the reader, may see that the magical word that has preoccupied him—*paralysis*—describes considerably more than Father Flynn's physical debility. In the final story of *Dubliners*, "The Dead," the word "dead"—that final paralysis—may refer not only to those faithful departed, but to their survivors; in this first story *paralysis* is applicable both to the priest (it has become his *rigor mortis*) and to those who mourn him, perhaps even his young friend in his interpretive dilemma or even the reader. Upon reflection we are meant to see that it is epidemic in Ireland's capital.

Like most of Joyce's work, "The Sisters," is about transcendence, in this case how a young boy wishes to elude the authority of elders who unwittingly inhibit his spiritual and intellectual growth, who are instructive only as negative examples. His impatience indicates that his uncle and Mr. Cotter are antagonists, a class eventually to be joined by the sisters of Father Flynn and perhaps the priest himself. More than age, what distinguishes the boy from the others is a condition of mind: the boy knows he knows little and seeks to arrive at understanding through inquiry, while the others think they know and obviously do not, long ago having given up the search for meaning. He is open to learning and experience; they are not. A condition of mind such as the elders have could be called *paralysis,* though, ironically, he will approach no nearer the truth than they. Still, his struggle to interpret is more noble than their acquiescence.

Gnomon is the second key word on the first page of "The Sisters," meaning, as the *OED* tells us, both a parallelogram with a smaller parallelogram missing in the upper right-hand corner and, second, the pillar of a sundial, which tells time by casting part of a circle into shadow. One should give more credence to Euclidean usage, since the boy's understanding is probably restricted to that, but Joyce surely knew that in both definitions the missing part is what is important, either as a space that defines a geometric shape or as a shadow that indicates the time of day. For this word *gnomon* I claim more than my predecessors, because by perceiving gnomonic principles at work, readers can gain new insight into character, structure, and narrative technique—not in all of Joyce's texts necessarily, but in enough of them to warrant systematic examination of these principles. Joyce probably knew that in Greek the word means "indicator."

Upon reflection, a reader might first be struck with the gnomonic nature of the story's language: it is elliptical, evasive, sometimes mysterious. A mystery is there to be uncovered, but boy and reader will be frustrated by language in their attempts to solve it. We do know that it concerns the priest's vocation, his apparently forced retirement due to the effects of paralysis (however that is defined), and the exact nature of his friendship with the boy, for whom all this is an area of experience perpetually cast in shadow. He seems totally dependent for information on his elders (who won't knowingly cooperate), just as the reader is on the text. Candlelight on a darkened blind (a geometrical form partially cast in light) may tell the boy that the priest is dead, but that will hardly be an issue. Too many pieces are missing from the puzzle for him to see the picture clearly. Even when important pieces are filled in, such as at the story's end, neither boy nor reader is party to any epiphany.

Gnomonic language works as follow: if the boy eschews dictionary meanings, unsympathetic characters in "The Sisters" misuse words and fracture sentence structure. Associated with their narrative style is the ellipsis, which presents hiatuses of meaning that can only be filled in by readers or listeners. The tiresome, pipe-puffing Mr. Cotter, speaking of the dead priest, says there was "something queer . . . there was something uncanny about him. I'll tell you my opinion . . . ," thus producing spaces in meaning while he hints at a clerical weakness he cannot or will not articulate. Even the boy falters at one point, when comparing the atmosphere of his mysterious dream to Persia. Like us, he is baffled by these holes in meaning: "I puzzled my head to extract meaning from his [Cotter's] unfinished sentences."

Questing characters in *Dubliners* are frequently assaulted by something I call a "tyranny of triteness," that is, the vacuous language or malapropisms associated with the people who await them at their destination. In "The Sisters" the boy hears ritual dialogue and misnomers like "the *Freeman's General*" for "the *Freeman's Journal*," "rheumatic" for "pneumatic" wheels. These signs of defective language are appropriate to the conversation's subject—a defective priest. Father Flynn "was too scrupulous always," Eliza says. "The duties of the priesthood was too much for him. And then his life was, you might say, crossed." (These hollow phrases, pumped so long for meaning by the critics, are meant to evoke laughter in the reader as they must have in Joyce.) Speaking at cross purposes, the aunt says, "He was a disappointed man. You could see that."

This exchange occurs as part of a ritual dialogue of condolence that Joyce must have heard at funerals or wakes. It is the gesture that is important, for the ritual words themselves are not really vehicles for communication. The dialogue begins with the aunt saying, "Ah, well, he's gone to a better world." One expects to learn nothing, yet the shocker comes when the sisters deviate from traditional inanity to reveal information about their brother that the priest would have wished left unsaid. This the boy must try to evaluate, but the story's final ellipses prevent readers from gauging his success.

So far we have discussed "gnomonic" language: ellipses, hiatuses in meaning, significant silences, empty, ritualistic dialogue. *Gnomon* is also the primary negating force in *Dubliners,* which is why there is continual emphasis on emptiness, incompletion, solitude, loneliness, shadow, darkness, and failure, which so affect the lives of the characters and allows subtle expression of Joyce's political views. Dubliners seek to fly by nets erected to keep them down. Here one of the chief advantages of textual ambiguity emerges: stories may achieve greater depth and complexity and yet seem simple enough to have broad, popular appeal. But by employing the subtle symbolist technique of suggestion rather than commentary, Joyce also could better fulfill his mission as a subversive artist. Readers alerted to the theme of ambiguity from the first page of *Dubliners,* "trained" to read the stories skeptically, could feel more deeply the political impact they contain. In theory the author then need not fear censorship because libelous thoughts are in the reader's mind, not in the text. Gnomonic ambiguity thus has the effect of enlisting a reader as co-creator in the production of meanings that are in harmony with the author's political intentions. This subtle alliance of politics and language helped Joyce to evoke the odor of corruption that hangs over his stories, to point the finger at the forces of oppression, and still to evade the consequence. *Dubliners* is often most eloquent in its silences.

Joyce must have been well instructed in the dictionary meanings of *gnomon,* because the concept is relevant to most of the major concerns of *Dubliners.* It points to what is missing, suggesting that these missing things are characteristic of the whole of Dublin life at a significant *time* in its history. (Here the sundial meaning of the word is applicable.) Readers are thus urged to examine the implications of what is missing, an approach taken with rewarding results by Hugh Kenner and Wolfgang Iser. In general, *gnomon* indicates how selective examples, such as the characters of *Dubliners,* define life in their city, how shadows illuminate presences, how abnormality can define the normal. The first sentence of "The Sisters" describes the hopelessness of Father Flynn's physical condition by saying that his time is growing short: "it was the third stroke." Immediately thereafter we are told that the school term is over—"it was vacation time," which here denotes free time within a school calendar and may hint at the story's theme of freedom and bondage. In the night a rectangular window is lighted in the priest's house, and if he is dead two candles will illuminate his head, while his feet are cast in relative darkness. If some words or silences are significant, clichés like "*I am not long for this world*" are thought "idle," gnomonic in their vacancy of meaning, just as the priest was partly dead in his life. All this play on light and shadow, presence and absence, is set forth in the first half page of "The Sisters."

As we read along, the word *gnomon* suggests additional possibilities: the boy lacks direction and guidance; he is told to box his corner as if his life had geometric shape; like the story his dream is open-ended; he usually sits in the corner of the priest's room. Father Flynn lacks a whole chalice, an intact vocation, muscular coordination, a confessor to absolve him, an appropriate vehicle in which to revisit the house of his youth. His mourners "gazed at the empty fireplace" in his room; the fallen chalice contained nothing. An obsolete meaning of *gnomon* is "nose" (*OED*), the cavities of which Father Flynn attempts to fill with snuff, though the greater part falls on his vestments. Boy and priest are counterparts as failed clerics, a small corner in the geometric shape of the church in Ireland, but one of real significance. Like their fellow Dubliners, they are gnomonic in their needs, gnomonic in their representativeness, and their story is gnomonic in that the precise description of their problems and the remedies thereof are left to the reader.

The third key word in the opening paragraph of "The Sisters" is *simony*, the buying and selling of ecclesiastical preferment. If *paralysis* describes the moral and physical condition of Dubliners, given their need for freedom, transcendence, and fulfillment, and *gnomon* reemphasizes these absences at a particular time in history, then *simony* too must be stretched to relevance. It points to corruption in high places and illegitimate ecclesiastical authority as primary obstacles hindering the peoples' fulfillment. Thus the first two terms describe the condition, telling the reader how to arrive at meanings deeper than the textual surface, while the word *simony* places the blame squarely where Joyce thought it belonged—on institutions and their representatives who barter what is a sacred right. Ambition, energy, free will, revolutionary zeal—these forces played no role, and could not, Joyce thought, in a city and country where centuries of political and religious oppression had caused a general paralysis of mind and will. Transcendence came only through death or emigration.

Simony reinforces *gnomon* and *paralysis* as a thematic key for understanding the story's central problem—what the boy and priest meant to each other. The term may be a broad paintbrush for church walls in Ireland, but it also works on the individual level. Father Flynn's own indoctrination program could in part have had personal gain as its motive; having cracked a chalice and lost a vocation, whatever guilt he might suffer could possibly be expiated by providing a clerical replacement. Spiritually, says Thomas E. Connolly, Father Flynn "has become a remainder after something else is removed, a gnomon." If, in addition, he is "not all there"—mentally as well as physically incapable of coordination—this defective priest, who is, after all, defined in terms of vocation, might from impure motives be capable of seeking a replacement for himself. The boy's preoccupation with *simony* might indicate an awareness that this trap has been evaded, but he too suffers from a kind of gnomonic vacancy in terms of vocation and experience.

The boy's dream of the priest trying to confess to him may be the beginning of the boy's awareness of impropriety. To hear the priest's confession is to accept the priestly vocation. Though this happens in a dream, he is aware of coercion and feels his "soul receding into some pleasant and vicious region," where, unwanted, the priest follows. We cannot know whether or not the priest has committed the sin of simony, but his young friend is definitely suspicious that he has been coerced by an old teacher who, at the least, has charged a tuition in snuff.

If "The Sisters" is seen as a geometric structure, then one part of it will always remain in shadow. Indeed, the elusive title suggests that meaning will be displaced. Gnomonic interpretation must thus involve speculation about textual meaning, and what follows is mine: If Father Flynn has sought to bind his novice, he has probably freed himself instead; if he has wished to indoctrinate him, it is surely the example of what he became that made the more lasting impression. Whatever transcendence the youth has gained, it involves not religion but a deeper knowledge of what it is to know. Like the boys in "An Encounter," and "Araby," or Little Chandler in "A Little Cloud," the price he pays for such rude instruction will be a sense of humiliation that will not soon fade. All of them have sought light, positive images, and have been taught by negatives, shadows, and incomplete geometric shape instead of the whole one. The last sentence of "The Sisters" describes Father Flynn in the confession box; like the coffin that will contain him, it is a rectangular shape now in shadow, now in light. The door is opened to reveal him laughing to himself, but what precisely causes this laughter, what it means, or what its consequences are for his vocation will remain forever in doubt. The story's final ellipses do leave space for our minds to focus on unspoken implications, but if the reader must supply the missing pieces, can the picture ever look quite the same to any two observers? . . . Essentially the question involves discussing where meaning resides in such a process and how it occurs—whether predominantly in the text, or in the reader's mind, or in the dialectical interrelationship.

Recently Colin MacCabe has said of *Dubliners,* "There is no single message inscribed in the code and the meaning of the text is produced by the reader's own activity. . . ." Furthermore, "The splitting of the subject is achieved through the accentuation of the split between enunciation and enounced. This is effected in the text of *Dubliners* by those moments when the reader is no longer assured in his position in the enounced and thus experiences his own discourses as enunciation, as a process of production." Although MacCabe approaches this subject from an angle different from mine, he seems essentially correct in describing what Joyce probably thought he was doing in his experiment with meaning.

Jacques Derrida and J. Hillis Miller told similarly skeptical views about the possibility of meaning occurring in reading. Miller has said: "all language is figurative at the beginning. The notion of a literal or referential use of language is only an illusion born of the forgetting of the metaphorical 'roots' of language. Language is from the start fictive, illusory, displaced from any direct reference to things as they are" ("Tradition and Difference"). All readings are thus misreadings; we are left with fragments of a truth we can never see whole. We cannot therefore speak of validity in interpretation, but only of the persuasiveness of readings, a relative concept. Although Miller does not write about the first page of *Dubliners,* he would probably sympathize with Joyce's strategy for teaching skepticism there, noting that the italicized key words are basically indecipherable because they have private meanings and associations as well as dictionary definitions that are slippery and loose.

In opposition to deconstruction is E. D. Hirsch, Jr., who made an important distinction between "meaning" and "significance" in *Validity in Interpretation*: that textual meaning cannot be separated from authorial intention, whereas significance may vary with the reader; in *The Aims of Interpretation* he reaffirms that "a text can be *interpreted* from a perspective different from the original author's. Meaning is understood from the perspective that lends existence to meaning. Any other procedure is not interpretation but authorship." Hirsch goes on to say that "Every act of interpretation involves, therefore, at least two perspectives, that of the author and that of the interpreter. The perspectives are entertained both at once, as in normal binocular vision. Far from being an extraordinary or illusory feat, this entertaining of two perspectives at once is the ground of all human intercourse."

Hirsch is persuasive in his defense of the traditional scholarly methods used to determine authorial intention. However, he seems not to have had Joyce in mind, for the central question for us here remains: Is critical relativism not justified where authorial intention can seldom be established and where the author himself subscribes to relativism? Yet even if Joyce favored textual ambiguity, it would of course be a mistake to conclude that authorial intention can never be established, or that Joyce never had a dominant message in mind in any particular statement, or that evidence, logic, authoritative reasoning, and judgment can do more than reinforce our own perspectives.

This brings us to a consideration of what seem to be problems in advocating the position that Joyce's texts were generally designed to reflect multiple meanings. One problem is that of authority. If interpreters of Joyce are caught up simply in MacCabe's "process of production," reading texts such as we have described from ever differing perspectives, how is it possible to distinguish between more or less plausible interpretations? Is it ever possible to state categorically that a Joyce text means x or y, or must one continually be diffident about meaning?

As early as 1965 Fritz Senn attached importance to the opening of "The Sisters" as forecasting the experimentalism to come in Joyce's work. Recently, in an important article, he emphasized the necessity of skepticism in reading, questioning "how we, as Joyce readers, when we could benefit from such a unique education in applied skepticism [as is found in Joyce's texts], can still be as dogmatic in our own practical performances as in fact we are." Senn urges critics to become less assertive, more aware that whatever evidence can be found for one interpretation, equally forceful evidence can always be found to contradict it. Among other things this suggests that no real progress has been made in understanding Joyce's texts since their publication; that criticism is only a game where no player really has an advantage; that all we can hope for is a fresh, interesting perspective in a discipline (?) where little or nothing of importance can ever be known.

But common sense tells us this is false, that we are much more knowledgeable, more sophisticated readers of Joyce than ever before, in large part thanks to the scholarship and rigor of traditionalists, and in part thanks to progress in the editing and publication of manuscripts and definitive texts. No other term but *progress* will do to describe that process by which we are continually able to learn new things about writers such as Joyce. The more we learn, the greater is our authority as readers and the more likely it is that our dogmatism will on occasion be justified. If Fritz Senn were to assume a dogmatic tone, I would listen respectfully.

The issues raised here about how meaning occurs in Joyce will never be settled to the satisfaction of many interpreters of texts, but they should be considered in depth by those who advocate an easy relativism, perhaps not having worked their way through the subtleties of works like Wolfgang Iser's *The Act of Reading*.

Joyce surely taught us to be skeptical about language, addressing the question most directly and humorously in *Finnegans Wake*, where, with mock seriousness, he says that although we "may have irremovable doubts as to the whole sense of the lot, the interpretation of any phrase in the whole, the meaning of every word of a phrase so far deciphered out of it [the hen's letter], . . . we must vaunt no idle dubiosity as to its genuine authorship and holusbolus authoritativeness." But in the face of this persistent attitude toward meaning, and our uneasy feeling that too much depends upon our response to the text and too little on the text itself or authorial intention, readers have no alternative but to be skeptical about Joyce's skepticism and to attempt to avoid the fallacy of imitative form in interpretation. We know intuitively that "The Sisters" is not about life in an Eskimo village, but at what point would we become intolerant of a brilliant espousal of that thesis? Obviously we have no recourse but to attempt to limit the range of possible meanings; good interpretation has to reject implausibility. Fortunately, Joyce helps us to do that too. Returning to the paradigm of our story, *gnomon* indicates that meaning is open-ended, but *paralysis* and *simony* are important keys to thematic limitation in interpretation.

Boy and reader in "The Sisters" seem to follow a parallel course in their struggle with meaning, but this is actually an illusion. The boy interprets the world as text and the reader the text as world. A sophisticated reader, recognizing the self-reflexive qualities of the story, can also read the text as text and consider its playfulness, but whereas there is no limit to the range of readers who may read the story, there is only one boy, and his level of sophistication can be established within a narrow compass. Though he narrates, he cannot read the text, nor can he be responsible for the range of possible meanings there. Though obliged to read the world as text, he cannot read the world as world, and, denied a glimpse at that epiphanic moment, the reader cannot know at the story's end how much the boy has learned about his world or even what the maturer narrator knows. Even if both decipher, the nature of their ignorance differs because of a time gap and the struggle of narration, differing as well from that of any reader.

In the end, a potential advantage lies with the reader, for the words of the text, regardless of slippery etymologies, do not change, while the boy-narrator must deal with shifting impressions based on incomplete information about a forbidden subject. Consciously or unconsciously, the narrator provides the reader with signposts to meaning, even if nobody in the text's world seems willing to render him a similar service.

The Dantean Design of Joyce's *Dubliners*

Mary T. Reynolds

The early critics of *Dubliners* saw the book as an example of realism, and the stories as typically *tranche de vie* writing. Gradually, however, it becomes clear that Joyce, as John Kelleher says, "may have regarded the surface story with an even more uncompromising realism than his critics have allowed," at the same time that he created successive levels of meaning by insistent symbolism. *Dubliners* was the first of Joyce's books to carry a suggestion of Dantean structure. The stories were written in the mood and manner of Dante's abrasive denunciations of faction-ridden Florence, the city Dante describes as "piena d'invidia," "full of envy" and every sort of iniquity. "Rejoice, O Florence," says Dante in the canto on Ulysses (*Inferno* 26), "in being so great that thy name resounds throughout Hell" (*Inf.* 26:1–3, trans. Singleton). Joyce's term "paralysis" is his metaphor for the "static lifelessness of unrelieved viciousness" that Samuel Beckett, writing under Joyce's inspiration, describes as the essence of Dante's Hell. *Dubliners* became Joyce's version of Dante's *Inferno*.

When Joyce sent the manuscript to Grant Richards in late November 1905, the first story, "The Sisters," was still in the form of its first publication in a Dublin paper edited by George Russell ("AE"), *The Irish Homestead*. But in the published version, as Jackson Cope discovered, the first story opens with the words that Dante set above the gate of Hell in *Inferno* 3: "There was no hope." Moreover, the final story,

From *The Seventh of Joyce,* edited by Bernard Benstock. © 1982 by Indiana University Press.

"The Dead," concludes with a vision of a frozen Ireland, a reminiscence of Dante's image of that frozen world "where the shades were wholly covered" ("la dove l'ombre tutte eran coperte"), from the final canto of the *Inferno* (34:11). The book's last sentence and its first sentence were written, as Professor Cope comments, in deliberate emulation of the *Divine Comedy*. The closing sentence of "The Dead" recalls frozen Cocytus, Dante's last image of despair: "His soul swooned slowly as he heard the snow falling faintly through the universe and faintly falling, like the descent of their last end, upon all the living and the dead." From *Dubliners* on, each of Joyce's works would carry a Dantean pattern.

The first of the *Dubliners* stories to be written were the three published in Russell's *Irish Homestead*: "The Sisters" in its first version, "Eveline," and "After the Race." The revision of "The Sisters" came very much later. Whatever Dantesque implications we find in the themes and arrangement of the stories must reckon with the belatedness of that revision, which made the theme of simony the central focus of the book as a whole. The fourth story was "Hallow Eve," for which no manuscript has been found except in the final form as "Clay." However, there was an earlier form of this story for which we do have the manuscript fragment that indicates the story's central focus to be a family gathering at holiday time. The discarded story carried the title "Christmas Eve." The first appearance of a Dantesque pattern in *Dubliners* is—whether by deliberate design or by a chance inspiration later amplified—in this change. Joyce discarded Christmas and gave his new story the ambiance of Halloween, thus introducing a fortune-telling motif that reflects Dante's *Inferno* 20, the canto of the soothsayers. The parallel is present not only in the predicting of future events in "Clay" but also in the witchlike appearance of Maria, which clearly owes something to the presence of another virgin in *Inferno* 20, the prophetess Manto, "la vergine cruda" (*Inf*. 20:82). Joyce took a new direction, it is now clear, with the writing of the fifth and sixth stories. Thereafter he wrote very fast, and brought the collection to its first-stage conclusion by December 4, when the complete manuscript was first sent to Grant Richards.

It seems, however, that the Dantean conception as such—the realization that his stories put together might form a narrative pattern similar to the scheme that makes Dante's *Inferno* a drama of passion and action, shaped as a moral critique of society—first entered his mind as early as March 1905. This was the month in which he finished chapter 18 of *Stephen Hero*. As originally written this chapter began with an episode deliberately constructed as a detailed parallel to *Inferno* 15, a parody of Dante's portrayal of Brunetto Latini. This has been thought of as a separate chapter, having been so labeled by Theodore Spencer because of a misinterpretation of Joyce's markings in the manuscript at MS pages 609 and 610. Joyce at this time apparently intended to use his pastiche of *Inferno* 15 as an episode in the final chapter of the revised *Portrait of the Artist*. At some time after 1907, and probably closer to 1911–12, he wrote in red crayon at the bottom of the page, obscuring four lines of his manuscript, "End of second Episode of V." (He also added the four lines to the margin of the next page, writing "Chapter XVIII" at the top of the page.) Thus when he says he has finished chapter 18, in a letter of March 15, 1905, Joyce is referring to a much longer piece of work. Significantly, this was a chapter of *Stephen Hero* that dealt with Dante and Aquinas, and it described a work, a critique of society, to be written by Stephen Daedalus. The terms used fit both the *Inferno* and *Dubliners*.

It is thus possible to say with confidence that Joyce's symbolic mode, which appeared in published form for the first time in *Dubliners*, must be recognized as an aesthetic decision closely connected with his judgment in favor of a Dantean matrix. When the titles are set in parallel columns showing both the order Joyce assigned to the stories in the book and the order of their composition, a new light is thrown on the last six stories Joyce wrote for the book. They are, in order: "Araby," "Grace," "Two Gallants," "A Little Cloud," "The Dead," and finally the massive revision of "The Sisters." These are the stories most plainly and specifically associated with cantos of Dante's *Inferno*, although each of the fifteen stories has its Dantean counterpart.

Another set of parallel columns, showing the order in which Dante placed sins and sinners in his *Inferno*, will allow the titles of the *Dubliners* stories to be arranged to show the Dantean moral order of Joyce's book. It is not Dante's precise order, but it shows a very close "fit" of the stories to the stages in his moral hierarchy. The result is a catalog of moral death, every story in *Dubliners* being matched with an episode in the *Inferno* either by subject matter or incident.

Let us examine this Dantean order of the stories. Joyce specifically described his ordering principle as a chronology from childhood to "public life." There is in "Araby," the third story, a strong reminiscence of Dante's *Vita Nuova*; the story thus becomes preeminently a little narrative of love, and its position at such an early stage in the book is surely related to the comparable position of the immortal Francesca in Dante's great love story in *Inferno* 5. Eveline, the heroine of the fourth story, is an indecisive character incapable of making a positive decision; she thus would fit the lukewarm sluggard who made the great refusal, "il gran rifuto," and was thereby condemned forever in the vestibule of Hell in Canto 3. An example of prodigal waste, which Dante the pilgrim saw paired with avarice in *Inferno* 7, is found in Joyce's fifth story, "After the Race."

The story "Counterparts" is Joyce's equivalent of *Inferno* 8, the canto that depicts Dante's Fifth Circle and its wrathful sinners. Farrington is the epitome of the violent man: "A spasm of rage gripped his throat," "His heart swelled with fury," "His fury nearly choked him." At the end of the tale we find that "he jumped up furiously," seized a walking stick, and beat his child, "striking at him viciously." No one is killed, but in his raging frenzy Farrington would also qualify for the Seventh Circle of the murderers, *Inferno* 12:49.

The mortal crime of suicide, punished in *Inferno* 13, has its turn in "A Painful Case." Sodomy, the matter of Dante's fourteenth and fifteenth cantos, is the subject of "An Encounter." With "The Boarding House," which was the first story written as an element in the Dantean pattern, we enter Joyce's equivalent at Malebolge, that vast expanse of hell where the fraudulent are found. Mrs. Mooney, the "Madam" who "deals with moral problems as a cleaver deals with meat," is quite clearly one of the panders of *Inferno* 18. In "Two Gallants" the seducers of *Inferno* 18 are seen in action, and the pairing of Joyce's two stories in the sequence of *Dubliners* seems to be an intentional reflection of Dante's linking of these two groups of sinners.

The simoniacs of *Inferno* 19 are represented in *Dubliners* by two stories, first in the new version of "The Sisters," with its explicit and fearful vision of the simoniac priest enticing the young boy into "some pleasant and vicious region." The story "Grace" is Joyce's classic portrayal of simony. It is a dramatic and unambiguous statement of the Irish clergy's exchange of spiritual benefits for worldliness and gain.

As we have noted, the story of Maria, the heroine of "Clay," turns on fortune-telling, a parallel to Dante's description of the soothsayers in Canto 20. "Ivy Day in the Committee Room" deals with grafters, the Dublin ward heelers whose corrupt maneuvers are the equivalent of the evil for which the barrators are punished in *Inferno* 21.

The eighth story, "A Little Cloud," takes its title from *Inferno*

26:39: "si come nuvoletta." This is Dante's simile of the little cloud, by which he describes the flame hiding Ulysses and other false counselors found in this region of hell. Ignatius Gallaher, whose fraudulence is stressed and whose bad counsel has helped to damage the life of Little Chandler, is described as similarly hidden, "emerging after some time from the clouds of smoke in which he had taken refuge." The story of Gallaher, suitably adjusted by Joyce, resembles a capsule history of the protagonist of *Inferno* 26: "Of course he did mix with a rakish set of fellows at that time, drank freely and borrowed money on all sides. In the end he had got mixed up in some shady affair, some money transaction: *at least that was one version of his flight*" (italics mine). The last words remind the reader that Dante in this canto invented a new version of the story of Ulysses. This was a sequel to the Homeric account, a last voyage that Dante describes as a "mad flight," "il folle volo," in *Inferno* 26:125, and then again as "il varco folle," "the mad flight," in *Paradiso* 27:82.

The thirteenth of Joyce's stories, "A Mother," shows the disruption created by the greedy Mrs. Kearney. Her quarrelsome nature makes her a classic example of the fomenters of discord whom Dante placed in *Inferno* 28.

The last story of *Dubliners*, "The Dead," has its correlative in the final cantos of the *Inferno,* where we find the traitors buried in the eternal cold of frozen Cocytus. Dante shows us examples of traitors to family, traitors to guests, traitors to benefactors, traitors to their country: all aspects of betrayal that can be found in the thoughts and actions of the protagonist of "The Dead," Gabriel Conroy. Joyce's setting, a Christmas feast, makes play with food as dramatically as Dante's tale of Ugolino portrays starvation, thus suggesting an ironical inversion of *Inferno* 33. The central figure at the feast is Gabriel, and Gabriel is punished, in the final incident with his wife that climaxes the story, as a reprisal for having sinned against his kinfolk and his country. The story, as John Kelleher has shown, is a ghost story. Gabriel ridicules his middle-class forefathers, to whom he owes his education and his present position as a well-to-do Catholic teacher in Protestant-dominated Ireland; they punish him for his unthinking temerity. He denies his country: "Well, said Gabriel, if it comes to that, you know, Irish is not my language." When baited by one of the guests, Miss Ivors, he retorts in a similar vein but even more strongly: "O, to tell you the truth . . . I'm sick of my own country, sick of it!" As these indiscretions continue and multiply, Gabriel makes a disrespectful salute to the statue of Daniel O'Connell, who compelled the repeal of the Catholic penal laws. Such a denial of Gabriel's origins is a spiritual betrayal, which is seen also in his contemptuous thoughts of his aunts and his family. Most unforgivable is his disdainful jest about the hard-working ancestor whose starch mill brought the Conroy family to the economic security that Gabriel carelessly takes as his due—the middle-class respectability of a house in the very sanctum of Protestant Ascendancy Dublin, Usher's Island. Gabriel's joking account makes everyone laugh at the old man's horse, plodding round and round the hated statue of King Billy—William of Orange, conqueror of the Battle of the Boyne— just as the subject Irish for so many centuries were forced to trudge and toil in a meaningless round under their masters' rule. Thus, after his humiliating rejection by his wife, we find that Gabriel's soul "swooned slowly" in a vision of himself and all Ireland covered with falling snow.

Joyce has followed Dante in creating a moral structure that is not a precise reflection of Catholic doctrine. Dante used the seven deadly sins as the structure of his Purgatory, but not in his Hell. There are striking omissions from the Dantean list of sins, and his ordering of distinctions in the gravity of moral error, while not in conflict with doctrine, is his own. He considers flattery a graver moral fault than seduction, and simony more serious than either; he gives but little attention to pride and envy. Joyce saw that Dante had taken a moral and philosophical (basically Aristotelian) pattern, rather than a strictly doctrinal pattern or even a purely religious basis for his structure. Both Dante and Joyce see their inferno in the nonsectarian terms with which Father Foster describes the structure of the *Inferno,* "mainly as an outline of *human* evil drawn by human wit" [italics mine] ("The Theology of the Inferno"). Only the heretics and simoniacs in Dante's hell are "Christian" sinners, in the sense that their transgression implies the standards of a specifically Christian world—and even here, the chosen heresy is Epicureanism, a form of unbelief that does not necessarily presuppose Christianity.

In some such reading of the *Divine Comedy* Joyce must have found his warrant for creating his own imaginative pattern and his own hierarchy of moral depravity. His *Dubliners* comes closest to Dante's *Inferno* in the strong emphasis that Joyce places on the antisocial quality of injustice in human malice and fraud. Joyce's idea of *"frode,"* fraud, which is the governing design of thirteen cantos, is a close reflection of Dante's. Joyce's stories emphasize malicious injury *to one's fellow man.*

A central element of his design is the disposition to inflict injustice and injury, which is found somewhere in every story and is dominant in several.

But Joyce also follows Dante in allowing his narrative skills free rein. Joyce wishes to call the attention of his city to its moral condition, and to do this he produces a vigorous play of personality and dramatic action. Hence the mixture in his stories of good and evil, faults and mere weaknesses, humor and anger and pathos. They are full of ambiguities, such as the plight of Maria in "Clay," which is rendered through a fortune-telling game that is harmless in itself and dangerous only when a whole society falls prey to superstition.

The fifteen stories are epiphanies of frustration, "broadening from private to public scope," in the words of Harry Levin. Joyce's tripartite structure presents his city under the aspect of childhood, youth, and maturity, with three additional stories representing, as he said, "public life" in Dublin, and ending with the longer novella, "The Dead." Such a chronological arrangement permits Joyce to suggest, as Dante also does, a progression from the less culpable forms of moral failure to the most unregenerate evil. In Joyce's view, the evils of "public life" under Dublin's institutional masters represented a moral failure far more culpable because it was unconscious of wrongdoing and quite self-confident. The last four stories of the book are suffused with complacence. A venal ruling establishment is portrayed throughout the book, operating under clerical guidance in a simoniacal pattern that becomes increasingly explicit. Dublin life has become a frozen conformity under this perverted control. This is the angry vision that issued in Joyce's Dantean arrangements of the stories of *Dubliners*.

Berlitz Days

Hugh Kenner

> O, triste, triste etait mon âme.
> —VERLAINE
>
> *And trieste, ah trieste ate I my liver!*
> —*Finnegans Wake*

James Joyce, B.A., taught English in Trieste, where he had found something else you could do with an Irish degree.

A degree led most young men one of three ways: toward law, the route his friend Con Curran had taken; toward medicine, like his friend Gogarty; or toward the priesthood. The first two entailed expense on a scale the Joyce family could no longer think of meeting, though even so Jim had dabbled in medicine, which proved not to be his cup of broth. As for the priesthood, its rule is that God chooses you, and though visions of an illuminated name, "The Rev. James A. Joyce, S.J.," had at one time swirled in his head, Jim grew convinced that whatever the Roman priesthood might be it had not been chosen for him.

He had been chosen instead by the Priesthood of Art, a notion not incompatible in those days with inkwells and low bohemia. In France lapsed Catholics staffed the Symbolist Movement, questing for efficacious words of power. *Hoc est enim corpus meum* were words that claimed power to alter whatever reality underlay bread's unchanged appearances. Quite as potent might be, though Stéphane Mallarmé, some fit words for the azure Nothing at the heart of everything in a world mysteriously destined to terminate in a book. (*Tout, au monde,*

From *Renascence: Essays on Values in Literature* 35, no. 2 (Winter 1983). © 1983 by Marquette University Press.

existe pour aboutir à un livre.) Gazing on his inkwell, he saw it "crystal-line as consciousness, with at bottom its drop of shadows pertaining to 'let there be something' " (*l'encrier, cristal comme un conscience, avec sa goutte, au fond, de ténèbres relatives à ce que quelque chose soit*). So the Penman of *Finnegans Wake* inhabits The Haunted Inkbottle.

In Paris Mallarmé had lived by teaching English. He had learned it in order to decipher inscriptions by Poe, an incanting bard whose very name was embedded in the syllables of "Poète." Less formally, and unpaid save by esteem, he taught with "inexhaustibly subtle speech" a way for his visitors to regard the universe: as a dream. (Likewise, remarked one of them, the sea is summed up by a murmur in a shell.) Arthur Symons had attended his Tuesday evening seances at 87 rue de Rome, and is said to have taken Yeats there (useless: Mallarmé's French was subtle, Yeats's bad). It was Symons who filled Yeats's head with tidings of a new Sacred Book of the Arts: a conception the better calculated to arouse Yeats in that Mallarmé himself ascribed it to the Alchemists.

In November 1897, in *The Savoy,* Yeats published *The Tales of the Law,* a *fin-de-siècle* fantasy in which the monk-errant Owen Aherne, connoisseur of fine wines through which the light can pass to dye his long delicate fingers, has acquired the lost *Liber Inducens in Evengelium Aeternum* of Joachim de Flora, who prophesied the triumph of the Kingdom of the Spirit over the dead letter. Its first part, *Fractura Tabularum,* the breaking of the tablets, invites adepts to invert the Mosaic commandments, and its second, *Lex Secreta,* the secret law, "describes the true inspiration of action, the only Eternal Evangel."

If this "Joachim" has been worded with the aid of Blake, a spirit more exclusive than Blake's has interfered, too. For there exist a secret few, we learn, "elected not to live, but to reveal that secret substance of God which is colour and music and softness and a sweet odour." These have "no father but the Holy Spirit," and no midwife perhaps but Arthur Symons, or rather W. B. Yeats's misunderstanding of how Symons misunderstood the sayings of Mallarmé. Whatever its pedigree, by age nineteen James Joyce knew whole paragraphs of it by heart. It helped shape the conception of "Stephen Dedalus," whose purpose is "to live, to err, to fall, to triumph, to recreate life out of life." Stephen is defined in part by the 1890s, in part by being an Irish ex-Christian.

Here "Irish" is a word to dwell on, since it affects the words he can use and what happens when he uses them. Stephen Dedalus about

1902 may be heard exchanging civilities with his Jesuit Dean of Studies, an English convert, while his silent mind reflects that they have, in fact, no common language at all. So how can they partake in the one reality?

> The language in which we are speaking is his before it is mine. How different are the words *home, Christ, ale, master,* on his lips and on mine! I cannot speak or write those words without unrest of spirit. His language, so familiar and so foreign, will always be for me an acquired speech. I have not made or accepted its words. My voice holds them at bay. My soul frets in the shadow of his language.

The list repays glossing:

Home. An Englishman's was his castle, an Irishman's the shelter from which he might momentarily be evicted.

Christ. When he cuts his thumb on a bottle an Irishman does not cry "Chroist!" but "Jaysus!"

Ale. Metonymy for wholesome English custom, scattered through the language as in *bridal* (bride-ale); but in Ireland they prefer a porter allegedly discovered in the eighteen century by a man named Guinness who had burnt the hops by mistake.

Master. In England your teacher, your Saviour, or one before whom you are pleased to touch your forelock; in Ireland the owner of a pack of hounds or the racker of a pack of tenants.

Joseph Conrad, a distinguished pioneer in the twentieth century enterprise of subduing English from without, used to complain that no English word was a word, so entangled was it apt to be in historical, social, moral half-assertions. His example was "an oaken table," where "oaken" does so much more than specify a wood. Some attributes of an oaken table are moral.

That seems not easy to appreciate in England, and as late as 1973 an English amateur of linguistics could find Stephen Dedalus's fret "sentimental and self-pitying, not even forgiveable in an undergraduate." This was Anthony Burgess, whose novel *A Clockwork Orange* is peppered with made-up words like *Droob* and equipped with a glossary; but Burgess reasoned that despite a few local words such as *crubeen, drisheen, oxter, plain* (pig's foot, black pudding, armpit, beer) "we need no special dictionary to read Joyce's plainer works." True, we do not think we do, and so may not know if we are reading askew. When a writer must install himself in an alien system of words, the simplest semantic chords may turn dissonant ("He was densely distressed," wrote Conrad, as no native would have), and expressions he feels most comfortably in control of may be taking control from him. Joyce might have been describing some of W. B. Yeats's early difficulties.

> The woods of Arcady are dead,
> And over is their antique joy

—so run the first lines in Yeats's *Collected Poems,* verses he wrote at eighteen in the course of inserting himself in all innocence into the English literary tradition. The fingerprints of his reading are everywhere. "Arcady" would be a word he had from Keats, who found it in Milton. "Antique joy" remembers Marlowe's "antic hay" the way annotators gloss it. In pairing this poem, "The Song of the Happy Shepherd," with one called "The Sad Shepherd," he is following Milton's "L'Allegro," as decades later he would go to "Il Penseroso" for strong confirmation of his myth of the Tower. As for melodious shepherds, young Willie would have met them in "Lycidas," and further down on the page the phrase "optic glass" assures us he's looked a few pages into *Paradise Lost,* where he found Satan's shield likened to "the Moon whose Orb/Through Optic Glass the Tuscan Artist views."

There is even an Irish Connection of a sort. Yeats's opening words echo a stock Nationalist complaint that Ireland's woods too are dead: destroyed by the English, ran the tale, to deprive Gaels of concealment, though what in fact finished them off was a seventeenth century frenzy for exporting barrel-staves and fueling iron-mills. Never mind, the melancholy fact of deforestation will nestle snugly into a rhythm of Milton's and a phrase of Keats's, who invented Arcady's "groves": at his cost, though, that hardly a reader will recognize the vanished woods of Ireland.

So while W. B. Yeats was forming his first style, English stylists were determining what he could say with it. One result was to suffuse his Irish Eden with unreality. "Noon a purple glow," indeed!—not a Lough Gill noon, that noon, an *aesthetic* noon.

The spectacle of Yeats getting into an alien tradition only to be put to great trouble getting out of it again may have stiffened the resolve of James Joyce to remake the language from scratch. By 1914 he was exhibiting English (to the English) as a system in which, early on, you say things like "When you wet the bed first it is warm then it gets cold," which Yeats would not have identified as a hieratic utterance. Persisting in his concern with sacred books and their authors, Yeats scanned the horizons visible from the Tower he had rebuilt in the spirit of Axel.

"Why are these strange souls born everywhere today?" Yeats would be asking as late as 1922: he meant souls "with hearts that Christianity as shaped by history cannot satisfy." And:

> Why should we believe that religion can never bring round its antithesis? Is is true that our air is disturbed, as Mallarmé said, by "the trembling of the veil of the temple," or "that our whole age is seeking to bring forth a sacred book"? Some of us thought that book near towards the end of last century, but the tide sank again.

It was in the year Yeats dated those words that the firm of Shakespeare & Co., Paris, published a big blue book called *Ulysses,* in which a mocker modelled on Yeats's friend Oliver Gogarty mocks the freedom with which an earlier Yeats had identified sacred books: "The most beautiful book that has come out of our country in my time. One thinks of Homer." That is cruel in conflating two Yeatsian remarks, one of which had pertained to Lady Gregory's *Cuchulain of Muirthemne.* A book called *Ulysses,* though, yes, that does make you think of Homer, though there's no sign that Yeats ever thought it a candidate for sacredness.

But in 1905 *Ulysses* was seventeen years ahead. Back in Dublin Yeats was burbling of Sacred Books and rewriting yet again *The Shadowy Waters*; Oliver Gogarty was making ready to buy the kind of automobile you wore goggles to drive; Joseph Holloway's journal was accumulating reprobations of Synge's new play, *The Well of the Saints* ("unpleasantly plain speech"; "mixture of lyric and dirt"). In Gaelic League classes patriots stumbled through Gaelic; in Dublin Castle authorities recruited spies. Easter was not to explode for eleven years.

In Trieste, amid a mixture of idealism and dirt, James A. Joyce, B.A., high in rented quarters he had scant prospect of paying for, worked on stories by night, taught Triestinos English by day. The girl who'd come with him from Dublin was pregnant.

He taught English according to the new Berlitz system, which departed from centuries of custom in forbidding a teacher to use any language in the students' hearing save the one they were learning. It was modelled on the fact that French children learn French by hearing French, not from discussions of French in a meta-tongue, and it forced him to confront anew, idiom by idiom, "this language, so familiar and so foreign."

> —It is raining. You have brought an umbrella.
> —??
> —An um-brel-la.
> —??
> —(*pointing*): Um-brel-la.

With what banalities were his days not filled? "It is a fine day. It is not raining. You have not brought an umbrella. The cat sits on the mat. There is tea in the pot. This is a pot. There is tea in it. I shall pour you some tea." For this he earned 9½ pence an hour, and priceless experience.

For what other writer has confronted English conversation like that, from the ground up? It is not by the intentions of speakers but by forms of words that much of its silence is filled, and dialogue contrived to tell facts to readers of stories is apt to be false dialogue. There is no sign that Joyce valued his Berlitz experience at the time. It brought in pennies. At night he could write.

Mrs. Mooney was a butcher's daughter. She was a woman who was quite able to keep things to herself: a determined woman. Note the Berlitz discipline whereby the words that precede it help define "determined." *She had married her father's foreman and opened a butcher's shop near Spring Gardens.* Note the subject of both verbs. *But as soon as his father-in-law was dead Mr. Mooney began to go to the devil. He drank, plundered the till, ran headlong into debt. . . . By fighting his wife in the presence of customers and by buying bad meat he ruined his business.* Note the order of these two items; scandal exceeds bad meat. And fifty monosyllables in eighty-one words.

Such were nuances Joyce could isolate in the heat of watching them elude beginners amid only the simplest constructions.

One thing seemed oddly clear: that the language of any Sacred Book of the Arts was destined to be English. Mallarmé had written a treatise on English words, *les mots anglais,* and Yeats's eye for symptomatic detail did not fail to note an English dictionary among the few books in the room of Paul Verlaine (who located in it, somehow, "Erysipelas"). Who now could cast a colder eye upon English than an Irishman with Jesuit training? Skeat's Etymological Dictionary dated from the very year of Joyce's birth, and he had read it in the National Library "by the hour."

His first published fiction (August 1904: he was still in Dublin) was an unsettling little story called "The Sisters." The names of the sisters were Nannie and Eliza and they had a brother, a priest, now dead upstairs. Reading the story today in *Dubliners,* we may think to wonder why Joyce called it "The Sisters," so much is its narrator preoccupied with the dead man. Then, paying heed to the sisters, we may notice that though Eliza talks incessantly, Nannie, who's so hardworking she's "wore out," says nothing whatsoever. This may prompt us to remember the sisters in St. Luke's narrative (chap. 10), one of whom, Martha, kept conspicuously busy while Mary (who had "chosen the better part") preferred divine talk.

In St. John's gospel (chap. 11) we encounter these sisters again. They have lost their brother Lazarus, but since their guest is the Messiah the ending is happy: Jesus calls him back from the grave. (Dubliners are not Bible-readers, but the words of recall rang out from pulpits annually. "Come forth, Lazarus!" went a Dublin joke; but "he came fifth, and lost the job.") Joyce's story ends like the joke. Near the end all talk stops for everyone to listen. "I too listened; but there was no sound in the house." This brother lies in his coffin unresurrected.

That is one way to commence a sacred book, by keeping your eye on another one. J. M. Synge, too, got themes by converting biblical ones, and it may have been the unwanted resurrection in *The Shadow of the Glen* that prompted Joyce. Having met Synge and argued with him about dramaturgy in Paris in March 1903, he is unlikely to have missed the play's premiere on October 8 when they were both back in Dublin. It is on record that Joyce turned up when a new production was in rehearsal the next summer, just before he wrote "The Sisters."

"I am writing a series of epicleti—ten—for a paper," Joyce wrote to Con Curran of his plans at that stage, some time in mid-1904. With ten envisaged, it is no surprise if he turned to the New Testament for his promptbook. Its themes were, by homiletic convention, reenacted all the time among Christian people; scales falling from eyes, faith moving mountains, assemblies in upper rooms: any preacher could tell you, and did tell every Sunday, how you'd recognize such things in the life around you. And we note that Joyce didn't say "stories," accounts of happenings; his word, *epicleti,* pertains to his clarifications of what clergy took it upon themselves to clarify.

Epicleti would be "invocations": in the Eastern rite, though no longer the Western, callings to the Holy Spirit, to come down and transubstantiate the ordinary. Joyce's casual use of it in 1904 is one more indication that for the patterns of his first stories we should search the scriptures. The Priest of the Eternal Imagination was hewing close to the texts rival priests elucidated.

The "paper" he mentioned was *The Irish Homestead,* where his connection was the gentle AE, another connoisseur of Sacred Books. Its readers were interested in cooperative dairies, and in the issue of August 13, 1904, an early text of "The Sisters" competed with advertisements for cream separators and milk pumps. No one, we may safely guess, AE least of all, divined the story's model, in part because beginner's technique obscured it. The narrative progressed by flat statement:

> We sat downstairs in the little room behind the shop, my aunt and I and the two sisters. Nannie sat in a corner and said nothing, but her lips moved from speaker to speaker with a painfully intelligent motion. I said nothing either, being too young, but my aunt spoke a good deal, for she is a bit of a gossip—harmless.

In the version of "The Sisters" readers of *Dubliners* know, barely a sentence of this was left untouched from beginning to end; that paragraph, for instance, became,

> We blessed ourselves and came away. In the little room downstairs we found Eliza seated in his chair in state. I groped my way towards my usual chair in the corner while Nannie went to the sideboard and brought out a decanter of sherry and some wine-glasses. She set these on the table and invited us to take a little glass of wine. Then, at her sister's bidding, she poured out the sherry into the glasses and passed them to us. She pressed me to take some cream crackers also but I declined because I thought I would make too much noise eating them. She seemed to be somewhat disappointed at my refusal and went over quietly to the sofa where she sat down behind her sister. No one spoke: we all gazed at the empty fireplace.

This uncannily engages the reader's attention. "Eliza seated in his chair in state"—the chair her brother has vacated forever: while Nannie does the necessary work, Eliza has made the move toward dominance. It is she who bids her sister pour the sherry. Nannie always performs these practical actions, but Eliza never: something the story is no longer explicit about. Also the boy who had been explicitly "young" has become a lad self-conscious about the noise he'd make eating crackers. And emphasis on his gossipy aunt is withdrawn, to keep our attention on the talkative Eliza. We are left to notice these things— good Berlitz technique. Also, like the boy, we are made to feel that behind all that is perfectly explicit there is something we are not quite grasping.

We may guess at what went wrong with Father Flynn. He grasped that God did not choose him—perhaps out of nonexistence? And, prompted by the enigma of the title, we may even divine the story's scriptural model.

We need not. But if we do, it gives us two narratives to compare. Of Luke's Mary and Joyce's Eliza, the word-oriented women, we may note that whereas the Bethany Mary "sat at Jesus' feet, and heard his word," the Dublin Eliza chatters; as for the Dublin Nannie, the one who plays the biblical Martha's part and keeps busy, she is not silent because occupied but because gone deaf (and "it would have been unseemly to have shouted at her"). There is no Messiah present of any description. And for counterpart to the center of St. John's story, when Jesus before he undertakes the miracle challenges the bereaved, "Believest thou this?," we have someone who (as the boy does not divine) some years ago lost all belief. Father Flynn was found "sitting up by himself in the dark in his confession-box, wide awake and laughing-like softly to himself." Later he would give the boy instruction, less in Jesus' way than in the way of the Scribes, with emphasis on "books as thick as the *Post Office Directory* and as closely written as the law notices in the newspapers, elucidating all these intricate questions." That was a touch Joyce added in the revising.

Had anyone in 1904 read "The Sisters" to its bottom, there would have been an outcry against the *Homestead* to rival the *Playboy* riots. But no one noticed, nor was it noticed either that the next story by "Stephen Daedalus" (September 10, 1904) had for unwritten text "Follow me," words the gospels twelve times ascribe to Jesus. You'd follow Jesus to an ascetic life, but it's not to that life the sailor in "Eveline" has summoned an impressionable girl. What she has in mind is matrimony, meaning escape. What he has in mind . . . but we've no access to his mind.

Eveline Hill in the end does not follow this chap who calls himself "Frank": perhaps just as well for her if you ponder the improbability of a house await for a bride in Buenos Ayres (Joyce's twist on the "Hi

Breasil" of Irish lore, a good place beyond the sea). When she doesn't follow he leaves anyway, hardly the act of a man who is claiming his bride. And like the rich youth (Matthew 19) who also declined to follow, Eveline sorrows and will think for the rest of her life that it was by her own fault she missed something grand.

In "After the Race," his next *Homestead* story (December 17, 1904), "Stephen Daedalus" returned to the troubled Rich Young Man. Jimmy Doyle, too, at the end of his story is troubled, though not, like his scriptural prototype, because of any injunction to distribute his heritage to the poor. No, he's remorseful after a meaningless night he has spent losing much of it at cards to other youths who are already rich. This is the least of the stories because most dependent on a prototype the others permit you to miss. (*Richard Ellman* [James Joyce] *suggests another prototype, the victim of enchanted cards in "Red Hanrahan," a story Yeats had published the previous December. With Joyce all things are possible. But I'd guess that only in the grip of an extrinsic idea like transposing the Bible's Rich Young Man to Dublin would he have attempted a milieu he didn't now, the yachting set. He never did that again.*) Joyce said he meant to rewrite it but lost interest. After that his connection with the *Homestead* lapsed; not that implicit blasphemy was discerned, but there were letters of complaint. Readers of "Our Weekly Story" were accustomed to a positive note.

By the end of December 1905, in Trieste, the "Epicleti—ten" had become twelve stories, soon afterward fourteen, by 1907 fifteen, that nobody would publish. A printer in London balked at the taboo word "bloody," and at other details. The London publisher dropped out. Dublin next, where there was fuss about mention of pubs by name— might Davy Byrne sue? Also "bloody" still gave trouble. In 1910–12 the same publisher (Maunsell's George Roberts) who was gathering Synge's *Works* into four volumes, shifts and all, dithered and temporized. Joyce travelled all the way to Dublin, to no avail. A Dublin printer who'd manufactured 1,000 copies of the book invoked his saints and destroyed them by fire, Joyce heard, though that was an Irish Fact (they'd been chopped). Back in Trieste, he responded to word of fire with "Gas from a Burner," in which the printer explains:

> Ladies and gents, you are here assembled
> To hear how earth and heaven trembled. . . .
>
> . . . .
>
> Who was it said: Resist not evil?

I'll burn that book, so help me devil.
I'll sing a psalm as I watch it burn
And the ashes I'll keep in a one-handled* urn.

(*Dublin euphemism, for a chamberpot. Thus in Ulysses the loop of his
akimbo arm gets Nelson on his monument called "the one-handled adulterer.")

This very next lent I will unbare
My penitent buttocks to the air . . .
My Irish foreman from Bannockburn
Shall dip his right hand in the urn
And sign crisscross with reverent thumb
Memento homo on my bum.

Memento homo: "Remember, man, that thou art mortal:" the priest says
this on Ash Wednesday, marking each penitent's forehead with a cross
of sacred ashes. The ashes had been last year's Palm Sunday palms,
which commemorated the branches strewn before the Messiah as he
entered Jerusalem that last time, on an ass. Recipients of Gas from a
Burner were free to divine how Joyce's last entry into Ireland's chief
city had ended, ut implerentur scripturae, in what he deemed a crucifixion. He never returned.

Aside from "The Dead," an afterthought of 1907, the last two
stories to be written were "Two Gallants," in which a man puts in
time wandering the streets while another man is performing a seduction, and "A Little Cloud," in which a poet manqué confronts the kind
of word-man who gets ahead. In these we may glimpse the author's
first intimations of the Bloom and Stephen situations in Ulysses. Likewise we may catch in Gas from a Burner an early whiff of the big
book's parodic manner, something it does not explicitly flaunt until
the long, savagely travestied patriotic set-pieces of "Cyclops" proclaim
the sacred commonplaces of men as self-righteous as Roberts's printer.

Large systems of attention are coming together. It was after "Two
Gallants" and "A Little Cloud," at the end of September 1906, that he
thought of a story to be called "Ulysses," about the Dublin Jew on the
Clonliffe Road—Jim and his brother both knew him—who went by
the name of Hunter and had a wife said to receive admirers. It is clear
that he's no longer finding his plots in the New Testament; any sacred
book will do.

If "Ulysses," as Joyce later reported, "never got any forrarder
than the title," that may have been because it was overmuch like "Two

Gallants" in its focus on a man putting in time, waiting. For it can't
have been meant to encompass the events in the second half of the
Ulysses we know. The title, what could that bring to mind save a
wanderer awaited by a faithful wife? And the ironic point would have
been, an *un*faithful wife. A story about a man adrift, attending to
makeshift business, knowing he's being cuckolded, that's a *Dubliners*
story, with "Ulysses" for a title. It encompasses the matter of seven
consecutive episodes of *Ulysses*, "Calypso" to "Wandering Rocks,"
and given what later came of the conception we are unspeakably
fortunate it never got written. When midway through "Wandering
Rocks" we watch Bloom procuring for his wife the new book she's
requested, moreover a piece of porn by which he's taken when he sees
their life mirrored in it, we recognize the tang of a *Dubliners* ending.
(The world, said Mallarmé, exists to end in a book.)

With *Ulysses* growing somewhere in the back of his mind, Joyce
went on teaching, went on trying to get *Dubliners* published, and
labored to rework yet another book, of which earlier he had dashed
off one thousand dispensable pages: the story of his own early life.
This was ten years becoming *A Portrait of the Artist as a Young Man,*
after which fiction in English would never be the same.

> Once upon a time and a very good time it was there was a
> moocow coming down along the road and this moocow that
> was coming down along the road met a nicens little boy
> named Baby Tuckoo.
> His father told him that story: his father looked at him
> through a glass: he had a hairy face.

In the first sentence, three words we've never read before: we
absorb them. Then for "glass" we guess to read "monocle," a word
Baby Tuckoo wouldn't know. And "hairy face" says "bearded," a
decision we are put to the risk of making. We enjoy no position of
privilege with a helpful author–cicerone at our side. We are Berlitz
pupils, moving alert, inductively, substituting, comprehending. The
English language is something this Irishman will have us *watch* as it's
never been watched before. ("When you wet the bed first it is warm
then it gets cold": two hundred pages later the mind in creation is
likened to "a fading coal": ponder that correlation.) For a page and a
half we undergo a qualifying exam, until a row of asterisks inaugurates
familiar narrative: "The wide playground was swarming with boys . . ."

A Sacred Book ought to be shapely by canons Pythagoras could disclose, and on this five-parted work, his first extended unified composition, Joyce impressed systems of mathematic form. On the second page a mocking vengeful chorus—

> *Apologize*
> *Pull out his eyes*
> *Pull out his eyes*
> *Apologize*

pounds through Stephen's brain and silently diagrams on the page the *a-b-b-a* figure Greek rhetoricians called *chiasmus,* later exemplified by such expressions as "but her long fair hair was girlish, and girlish . . . was her face."

Chiasmus, though, is not confined to clauses. It is everywhere; the whole book is chiasmic, its left the mirror of its right, the even-numbered chapters, 2 and 4, set in correspondence with a vision of a woman at the end of each, and the diary fragments of the book's last pages reflecting the quick-cut glimpses of its first.

We may even wonder if such symmetry has a center. It has. The center falls midway among the four sermons which make up the middle part (of three) of the middle chapter (of five). What we find between the second and third of the sermons is exactly this:

> The preacher took a chainless watch from a pocket within
> his soutane and, having considered its dial for a moment in
> silence, placed it silently before him on the table.

Note "silence" and "silently"; note too a chiasmic pattern early in *Finnegans Wake,* which may be summarized,

> 1132 A.D. . . .
> 556 A.D. . . .
> (Silent.)
> 556 A.D. . . .
> 1132 A.D. . . .

Note also that *Finnegans Wake*'s middle chapter (of 17) is 9, the "Mime," near the middle of which we find

> . . . silent. ii. . . .

What does all this mean?

We may guess what it means in the *Portrait,* at any rate. *A Portrait of the Artist as a Young Man* borrows its title from Rembrandt, who painted his numerous self-portraits with the aid of a mirror. So imagine, arrayed,

{	0	||	0	}
Back-ground	Painter	Mirror	Painter's image	Background's image
Dublin	Joyce	Silence	Stephen	"Dublin"

Lo, chiasmus. The text places silence where Rembrandt's mirror is, because when the busy sounding world ends in a book it passes through print's looking-glass into a silent domain. Any book is silent, the silence of a sacred book uncanny.

So reduced, chiasmus seems a feeble joke to have given the Fabulous Artificer so much trouble. But all jokes are feeble, sufficiently reduced; so, Joyce would have us think, is the underlying structure of all we can know; a flaccidity of weltering coincidence, only arresting when enfleshed in rich meretricious multiplicity. The pun is mightier than the word.

By 1914 *Dubliners* was published, and *A Portrait of the Artist as a Young Man* was being serialized. Joyce had beaten out his exile and was uniting every wile he knew to tell at last the story of Ulysses, *sub specie temporis nostris*. When it was published in 1922, *Ulysses* was a new kind of book altogether, a Berlitz classroom between covers: a book from which we are systematically taught the skills we require to read it. The first response, shock, was like the shock you'd feel if you were suddenly put down where you hardly knew the language. In subsequent decades readers were learning how to learn. From Trieste, from Zurich, finally from Paris, the Irish Jesuits' most cunning pupil had silently made the literate world his classroom. The subject of study was the English Dean of Studies' native tongue.

Metaphors of the Narration / Metaphors in the Narration: "Eveline"

John Paul Riquelme

In the commentary on "Eveline," we shall examine Joyce's strategic placing of a simile in the story's final paragraph. I mention that placement now because it helps establish the continuity of the telling, despite the change in the grammatical person of the narrator. That continuity arises not from an invisible, impersonal narrator but from one willing to create similitudes. The narration's consistency, though, emerges not just through the continuing use of metaphorical language. Rather, it emerges because the metaphors create similar stances for narration, whether the narration is first- or third-person. Metaphor in "Araby" contributes substantially to the dissonant quality of the telling by emphasizing the difference between narrator and character. That dissonance and differentiation make the shift to third person less jarring than it might otherwise be. Like the simile at the end of "Eveline" and the later simile of the pearls at the beginning of "Two Gallants," the other metaphorical language in the middle stories tends to keep the narrator in the reader's view.

Metaphor in Joyce's fiction can also function structurally by giving the reader access to large rationales for the narration. Generally, the title rather than the language of narration contains this kind of structural metaphor. We have already seen the implications of the title of *Finnegans Wake* when treated as figures, both pun and metaphor. As I have interpreted it, that title focuses the reader's attention on the act of

From *Teller and Tale in Joyce's Fiction: Oscillating Perspectives.* © 1983 by the Johns Hopkins University Press, Baltimore/London.

writing as telling but also suggests the possibility that the storytelling bears a determinate relationship to the narrative's action. Although I would not overemphasize the larger implications of Joyce's titles in *Dubliners*, several of them are suggestive, particularly in their interaction. We have already formulated some of the relationships between narration and narrative using the title of the second story. The encounter is the narrator's with himself and ours with both narrator and character, as well as the boy's encounter with the old man, with literature, and with his own feelings about his companion. Robert Scholes has suggested that the title "Counterparts" can be taken in a similar way when he argues that through style Joyce has offered us "the opportunity—and the challenge— . . . of becoming . . . Joyce's counterparts." Scholes speaks of the reader's "complicity" "in the creative process," and he claims that by "entering the world of *Dubliners* we all acknowledge our Irishness." It is worth adding that in *Dubliners* Joyce is still only developing styles for creating the reader's complicity. The reader's active re-creative dialectical relationship with the text emerges more fully from the works following *Dubliners*.

While Scholes quite correctly stresses the sense of similarity implied in the word "counterpart," that word can also refer to something complementary that functions to complete. In this sense the reader is the teller's counterpart not only because the reading and the telling of Joyce's fiction are similar creative processes but also because the reader completes the teller's work. In these stories the teller is the counterpart of his characters sometimes because of a resemblance between them but more often because the teller's representations of consciousness complete in some way the characters' acts of mind. We have seen the teller's act of completion already in the stories told in the first person, in which the character's silence has been transformed into the narration presenting it. A related, though not identical, transformation occurs in the later stories whenever the narrator presents the character's mind in the narration's language. I shall deal further with the difference and the similarity between these two types of transformation in my commentary on the end of "Eveline." In "The Dead" the act of speaking *for* the silent and the inarticulate is inscribed in the narrative as well as in the narration when Gabriel Conroy speaks, however inadequately, *for* as well as *to* the people who attend his aunts' party. With regard to this story especially, Scholes is right to mention the relevance of the volume's title to the reader's involvement. By creating the possibility of that involvement, in "The Dead" Joyce begins to express, and allows us to recognize, the cultural consciousness linking past and present that we encounter repeatedly in the later fiction. Teller, reader, and characters of these tales are *all* Dubliners, and they are all related in various ways to the dead. We become members of an extended family created by the book. In his after-dinner speech Conroy speaks for and about the dead, with whom he ultimately associates himself. In their analogous acts of speaking, Conroy and the teller of his story are counterparts. But the titles of these stories, while significant as metaphors for the teller's and the reader's stance toward the narratives, do not call attention to themselves in the way Joyce's later titles do. Those later names point more obviously to structural principles of narration, as in *A Portrait*, where the structural principle involves the dual reference to both portrayer and portrait.

In "Eveline," the simile at the story's end depends for its effect on preceding strategies for presenting Eveline's thoughts. The story's style consists essentially of psycho-narration together with some brief instances of quoted monologue that are identified through the use of the exclamation point ("Home!") or the colon. The narrated monologue, toward which these other techniques, especially in combination, tend, also occurs here occasionally. . . . The lack of deictic references and exclamations [in the narrated monologue of "Eveline"] belies the feeling of immediacy and of alignment between character and teller that is possible with this technique. Overall, early in the story, we have *begin.* the impression of Eveline in meditation and of her process of mind as a logical, orderly procedure, though not a sophisticated one. But toward the end of the story, narrated monologue occurs more often, and the language of Eveline's thoughts becomes heightened. The teller renders *end.* one climax of Eveline's agitation in a particularly intense, comparatively extended passage of narrated monologue:

> She stood up in a sudden impulse of terror. Escape! She must escape! Frank would save her. He would give her life, perhaps love, too. But she wanted to live. Why should she be unhappy? She had a right to happiness. Frank would take her in his arms, fold her in his arms. He would save her.

After presenting Eveline's act of standing in affective terms, the narrator shifts first to an interior exclamation as quoted monologue and then to the narrated monologue. The remainder of the paragraph can be understood as the character's interior speech in first person and a combination of present and future tenses that have been translated into the third person, the past tense, and conditional expressions.

After this climax of style and story, a row of periods intervenes before the brief conclusion, which is narrated differently. In the conclusion, the narrator alternates, as earlier, between presenting scene and presenting Eveline's thoughts. But now those thoughts exhibit the emotional agitation of the climactic passage of narrated monologue. The narrator closes the story with a short paragraph in which he seems to withdraw completely from the character's perspective:

> He rushed beyond the barrier and called to her to follow. He was shouted at to go on but he still called to her. She set her white face to him, passive, like a helpless animal. Her eyes gave him no sign of love or farewell or recognition.

While the focus on action and on description in this paragraph might suggest impersonality, objectivity, and the withholding of judgment, the narrator's stance is *not* entirely impersonal. In his simile the narrator is not simply recording facts. Through the comparison, he expresses a judgment about Eveline's state of mind: that she has been reduced by her situation and by her own reaction to a helpless, passive condition. By comparing her to an animal, the teller does not suggest by any means that she is subhuman, simply that her condition is one of severe, paralyzing fear. The comparison takes on this *affective* connotation as the conclusion of an accumulating series of words and phrases indicating fear that fills the story's last two pages, not as a complete withdrawal from an affective presentation: "trembled," "terror," "distress" (used twice), "nausea," "frenzy," "anguish." Rather than withdrawing from the character's mind absolutely, the narrator has chosen to represent it in a new way that builds on and completes the earlier representations of her mind at the same time as it brings the story to closure.

The language of narration manages to work in at least two ways at once. While it expresses what the character's actions and feeling mean, it also announces through figuration its difference from any mode of thinking or speaking available to the character either in the narrative action or as a result of that action. We can read the shift in style as the narrator's demarcation of one limit for his own techniques in this story. Once he has brought the character gradually to a climactic state of frenzy, he can render that agitation only metaphorically, not by any seemingly more direct representation. As an admission that

Eveline's state of mind is beyond the reach of referential language, the act of shifting styles *itself* represents that state of mind which cannot be rendered adequately through psycho-narration, quoted monologue, and narrated monologue. This structural representation involves the two meanings of counterparts as both resemblance and completion. As a means of closure, the shift in style is appropriate in two ways. Structurally, it mirrors the change the character undergoes when she breaks off her previous communication with Frank and within herself. She indicates that change through the physical gestures of clutching the railing, setting her face to (that is, both toward and against) him, and showing no recognition. Since Eveline's turning her face toward Frank is also her rejection of him by setting the features of her face against him, Joyce can include the psychological within a physical description. (He does this again when he describes Gabriel's tears at the end of "The Dead.") The stylistic change also enacts the difference between character and narrator in a more definite way than do other aspects of the story. The difference recalls the contrast in the tales told in first person between the teller and the reticent character that is his earlier self. The act of representing in the final paragraph counters Eveline's refusal to give any "sign of love or farewell or recognition." The teller's stylistic farewell recognizes her state. But the resemblance to the narrating situation in the preceding stories is just that, a resemblance, not an equivalence. The boy's development is toward speech. Eveline's is toward silence.

Painful Cases

The narration of "Eveline" sets the mode for the eight stories of adolescence and adult life. In all these tales, besides frequently evoking the character's thoughts, the narrator always asserts his presence and his difference from the characters, but not obtrusively. He creates two effects at once; one of intimacy, the other of withdrawal. At the end of "Eveline" he assumes his last ambiguous position in the narration with particular subtlety and concluding force. Neither the representation of consciousness nor the narrator's separation from his characters is particularly surprising. But the combination can be, for its results in a strong tension and contrast within the narration. The narrator generally controls that tension by translating it into an orderly fluctuation of perspective, a modulation emphasizing now the character's view, now the narrator's, depending on the exact mix of techniques and diction.

But the tension is always there. It emerges most strongly when we feel in the modulations, as we regularly do, the narrator's dominance. We are dealing not simply with an antithesis between two wholly separate poles. Each position in the contrast possesses the potential for becoming the other view or at least for moving closer to that view, and, in so doing, for establishing a dialectical relationship. That relationship is our oscillating perspective.

We can put this potential in another way: the inner and the outer views are not absolutely segregated between the character and the narrator respectively. The overcoming of separation can develop out of either the narrator's or the character's pole of the contrast. In *Dubliners* the development of the character's view toward the narrator's occurs for the most part in the stories told in the first person. As we have seen, the boy's sense of himself moves toward coincidence with his own later judgment about himself, based, of course, on his earlier experience. In the middle stories, although some of the characters may come to realizations about themselves that narrator and reader share, a wide gap of sensibility predominates. The mergers of inner and outer views that seem possible in the third-person tales develop from the narrator's perspective. The simile in "Eveline" is a good example. The narrator's language allows the inner view so prominent in the story to nest within what seems ostensibly to be his outer view. This use of style does not yet achieve fully the oscillating perspective of *A Portrait*, with its radically ambiguous relationship between teller and character. But it is that perspective's immediate precursor, a crucial stage on the road to its development.

Without the curious first sentence of "The Sisters," there would seem little possibility that the superimposing of views in these stories could be developed further than the style of "Eveline." The creation of an oscillating perspective in third person narration seems especially unlikely. Joyce's ability to achieve it nevertheless is one of his great strengths as a writer. He presents it more fully than in "The Sisters" once he combines the two movements that have been largely separated in the first- and third-person stories: the shift of the character's perspective toward that of the narrator and the shift of the narrator's style toward one embodying the character's perspective together with his own. The narration of the middle stories never reaches that combination. Instead, by reiterating the narrator's difference from his characters, it prepares us for the change to tales of public life.

The particular combinations of techniques and choices of language in these middle stories deserve careful analysis. Because our primary concern is the overall development of the style toward techniques and visions enabling Joyce to write *A Portrait* and *Ulysses,* I shall limit myself, for the most part, to brief comments about the remaining stories. I shall treat in greater detail only "A Painful Case," the transition to the stories of public life. In general, the narrator maintains his distance by presenting the character's thoughts in ways that mark them as indisputably the character's attitudes. A number of the strategies from "Eveline" reappear, at times in slightly exaggerated ways. In "The Boarding House," although Mrs. Mooney's thoughts are presented at some length, we have little sense of immediacy in the presentation. While Eveline's mental processes are generally logical, though unsophisticated, Mrs. Mooney's are cold and calculating, essentially devoid of emotion except as a mask for self-interest. The colloquial, conventional, or cliché quality of the character's internal speech is often more extreme in the stories after "Eveline." For example, when Jimmy Doyle comments to himself that is companions are "devils of fellows" and that "this was seeing life, at least," no matter what techniques may be used for presenting thought with seeming immediacy, we feel strongly our own and the teller's difference from the character. In this story, the narrator reports the wonderfully muddled metaphors Doyle uses to characterize his own experience: "The journey laid a magical finger on the genuine pulse of life and gallantly the machinery of human nerves strove to answer the bounding courses of the swift blue animal." Doyle may be trying to fuse his body and mind with the car in which he is riding, but the teller is clearly not merging with his character's mind, the ungainly vehicle for his narration. "Clay" is the extreme case of thought evoked in conventional language in *Dubliners.* Often the ostensible representation of mind in that story would better be called a report of attitudes. The evocations of Maria's perspective are so flat and unelaborated that they seem little more than sense perceptions couched in vague, stilted language.

In the more complicated stories, "A Little Cloud" and "Two Gallants," both written late and inserted into the already formed collection, the metaphorical elements of the narrator's style differentiate his statements clearly from the character's internal ones. Like the simile of the pearls at the beginning of "Two Gallants," the narrator's language in "A Little Cloud" calls attention to itself vividly though not at great length. As Little Chandler walks the streets of Dublin on his way to meet Ignatius Gallaher for a drink, he passes through an area in which "a horde of grimy children populated the street": "They stood or ran in the roadway or crawled up the steps before the gaping doors or squatted like mice upon the thresholds. Little Chandler gave them no thought. He picked his way deftly through all that minute vermin-like life and under the shadow of the gaunt spectral mansions in which the old nobility of Dublin had roistered. No memory of the past touched him, for his mind was full of a present joy." This passage bears comparison with Stephen's walk across Dublin on the way to the university in which he associates what he sees with styles of language. By contrast, in "A Little Cloud" the interest of the walk for the reader is not what passes through the character's mind but the narrator's style for presenting what does *not* occur to the character. Here is one of those brilliant passages in these middle stories exhibiting sharply the opposition between teller and character. While Little Chandler ignores his present physical surroundings and their past, the narrator turns them both into striking, rhythmical language. The juxtaposition of high and low styles, the one evoking a possibly noble past, the other a grimy present, anticipates directly the contrasts of style and focus in *A Portrait*. The energy of this story is not in Little Chandler's mind, however immediately or distantly rendered, but in the mediations the teller employs to present the life that Little Chandler gives "no thought."

Another kind of contrast between teller and character emerges at the end of "Counterparts" in a conclusion resembling in certain ways the end of "Eveline." As in the earlier story, the concluding two pages are separated from the rest of the narration. The conclusion in both stories begins with a presentation of the character's thoughts followed by a focus on scene and action. But the shift is of different proportions and more extreme in "Counterparts." The presentation of thought is briefer; that of scene, action, and speech, longer. As in "Eveline," the character reaches a pitch of agitation (for Farrington a compound of frustration and anger, not fear) that accompanies a break in communication, this time as the father confronts and terrorizes his helpless son. But there are no similes or metaphors to announce and possibly to bridge the gap between inner and outer views, to modify the starkness of the shift to an external perspective. While the narrator's change in mode reflects again the failure of communication between characters, now it represents as well a more resolute turning away from the character's mind and a harsher judgment. The narrator can speak for the character's interior silence or turmoil in these stories, when he wishes to, but here he allows the character's actions to speak virtually for themselves.

In the symmetrical arrangement of the stories in *Dubliners,* "A Painful Case" provides the transition to the stories of public life, just as "Araby" and "Eveline" act jointly as the transition from first- to third-person narration. If we leave aside "The Dead" temporarily and consider the volume's shape before that story was added to the sequence, the large features of the symmetry are evident. What were originally the last three stories balance and, in certain ways, counter the first triad. "A Painful Case" carries the burden of transition by reversing some and duplicating other features of the earlier shift separating the first triad from the rest. As we have seen, "Eveline" ends with a change in style indicating the narrator's relative withdrawal from the character's mind, which the narration has prepared us for since early in the story. Her thoughts are largely a response to a situation she has not encountered previously, one that holds out the possibility of escape from Dublin. In Duffy's story, the movement of the narration is different. There is little report of thought at the start, much less than in the first pages of "Eveline." Within the story, the style develops gradually toward the intimate techniques of narrated and quoted monologue, which the narrator employs, then abandons, then employs again in a sustained way for the story's conclusion. Although the narrator does draw away partially from the character's perspective and from these techniques in the final paragraph, the swerve is not nearly as extreme as at the ends of "Eveline" and "Counterparts."

The increasing intimacy of narration within "A Painful Case" reflects the character's changing perspectives, ones that make the placement of this story as the last of the middle sequence appropriate. What little report of thought the narrator includes at first consists of a few references to the character's attitudes. The handling of these brief references suggests that Duffy no longer needs to think actively about the way he feels and lives. His life has become a routine that he controls rigidly. Consequently, at first the narrator has little fluctuation of habitual behavior and mental processes to report. Some of Duffy's attitudes and actions make the story a preamble for the ones to follow. We learn immediately that he lives in Chapelizod because he wishes to withdraw from Dublin. He desires to live as if he were not an inhabitant of either the city or its "mean, modern and pretentious suburbs." His disdain for the city prepares us for the teller's decision in the next three stories to adopt a distanced, ironic stance in relation to his characters and their world. Through another detail of Duffy's habitual thoughts mentioned early in the story, the narrator emphasizes the correlation between the character's withdrawal and a perspective for narration: "He lived at a little distance from his body, regarding his own acts with doubtful side-glances. He had an odd autobiographical habit which led him to compose in his mind from time to time a short sentence about himself containing a subject in the third person and a predicate in the past tense." Duffy's habit is reminiscent of *The Life of Giambattista Vico Written by Himself,* an autobiography in third person and past tense that Joyce would have known.

The mention of autobiography and the implied contrast between first- and third-person narration make the comparison between this story, the first three, and "Eveline" almost inevitable. While Eveline's final agitation is not amendable to direct presentation in referential language, the conclusion Duffy arrives at subsequent to his disturbing experiences consists of a self-conscious judgment that the narrator can report directly. The kind of judgment Duffy makes and even the act of judging contribute to the transition to the next stories. The contrast I am suggesting between Eveline and Duffy and between their stories concerns the characters' responses to crisis. By the time Eveline fails to board the boat with Frank, she has been virtually agitated out of thinking rationally. Duffy's crises do not affect him in precisely that way, though they do finally undermine his habitual modes of thought. Ultimately, Duffy begins to consider his own actions and thoughts critically when forced to by personal distress, arising because his familiar attitudes cannot cope adequately with his experiences. Inadequate, inept, familiar behavior and attitudes will be the narrator's continuing focus of judgment in the stories to come.

After sketching the regularities of Duffy's life in the first few paragraphs of the story, the narrator presents the character's mind more frequently and with increasing specificity. This increase corresponds to Duffy's growing tendency to be communicative as his relationship with Mrs. Sinico develops toward intimacy. As "little by little he entangled his thoughts with hers," the narrator gives us more of Duffy's thoughts. The narrator emphasizes Mrs. Sinico's role as catalyst for Duffy's thinking by first repeating nearly verbatim this statement about the entangling of their thoughts and then comparing the couple to a sensitive plant and its soil: "Little by little, as their thoughts entangled, they spoke of subjects less remote. Her companionship was like a warm soil about an exotic. . . . This union exalted him, wore away the rough edges of his character, emotionalised his mental life." In the paragraph in which the passage occurs, the narrator places himself temporarily at some remove from the details of his characters' attitudes by summarizing, in a series of iterative statements, the history of the private encounters between them. The actions and thoughts presented occur "often" (used twice), "little by little," "many times," "sometimes," and "more and more." Within the context of these iterations the teller inserts the similitude of soil and plant along with his judgment about the effect the relationship gradually works on Duffy's harshness.

At the end of the paragraph, the narrator punctuates the summary by shifting briefly to a more direct rendering of thought in the present tense, as if the statement by Duffy's interior voice were direct discourse: "We cannot give ourselves, it said: we are our own." This more direct rendering marks a moment of intensity in the characters' relationship. Although the sentence is the narrator's report of what Duffy hears his "strange impersonal" interior voice say, it also tells us what Duffy says to Mrs. Sinico just prior to her singular act that will end their affair. The narrator achieves the jointure between iterative and singular skillfully by allowing this specific example of Duffy's inner, and perhaps audible, speech to emerge from the otherwise sketchily presented discourses. The ambiguity in the narration by which the inner voice can be read as becoming audible during the characters' talks pinpoints the immediate context and the provocation for Mrs. Sinico's action. Her emotions, like his, are finally manifested as perceivable gestures. The interplay between man and woman, thought and speech, emotion and gesture, language and sexuality introduced in this paragraph only to be abruptly truncated is developed more fully, as we have seen, in Stephen's act of writing his villanelle in *A Portrait*.

As in several of the earlier stories, but unlike the presentation of the villanelle, in "A Painful Case" the narrator's act of storytelling stands in clear contrast to the character's actions. Like the boy in the first stories, Duffy usually keeps his thoughts to himself. During their conversations, Mrs. Sinico asks him why he does "not write out his thoughts." He responds, in effect, that he does not wish to expose himself to misconstrual. Instead of writing, he speaks his thoughts to her, only, in his opinion, to be wildly misunderstood. For Duffy, the experience confirms his general propensity not to try communicating and his specific one not to write. The narrator, however, does write out Duffy's thinking, including even his abandoning any significant, self-reflective mental activity. It is clear from those thoughts and from Duffy's actions that *he* and not his listener misunderstands the implications of his own statements. The remainder of the story concerns how Duffy comes to realize the meaning and effects his attitudes can have when he acts upon them, as he does with Mrs. Sinico. He finally discovers, too late to mend his error, that *he* has misunderstood himself and his companion.

Once Duffy "break[s] off their intercourse," he returns to the "even way of life" he established before meeting Mrs. Sinico. He maintains his interests in music and philosophy, but he writes "seldom" and avoids "concerts lest he should meet her." Stylistically, the narration also regresses. The movement of style in the story's second half parallels that of the first half: from little or no report of thought to a great deal of it. But in the latter half the shifts and contrasts of style are more exaggerated. As at the story's beginning, the narrator starts with a mediated presentation of Duffy's mind. Only now the references to thought are so attenuated as to be almost absent. It would be hard to call the style here psycho-narration, because the narrator does not present the character's attitudes explicitly. He can do without them, having previously established for the reader the nature of Duffy's mind. He merely mentions a few details of Duffy's life in summary together with a comment about "the orderliness of his mind." This phrase contains the only direct reference to consciousness in the narration concerned with Duffy's reestablished routine prior to his chance reading of the newspaper article. This segment of the narration suggests even more emphatically than before that Duffy's life has become so routine that he has to think hardly at all in order to continue his normal round of living. It also intensifies by counterpoint the effect of the greatly agitated thinking that occurs after Duffy reads the article. In Duffy's reaction to the article, the narrator presents the character's thoughts more directly and at greater length than earlier.

Like the thought reported as if speech that destroys the affair with Mrs. Sinico, the more direct presentation of consciousness in the story's last pages indicates a period of intensity in the character's emotional life. The length of the representation of mind and the prominence of narrated and quoted interior monologue, as well as psycho-narration in the conclusion, set it apart as special not only in this story but in the entire volume. Except for the final pages of "The Dead," Duffy's response to the article is the longest intense evocation of thought in *Dubliners*. The narrator interrupts the flow of thinking at length only once, to describe the scene at the pub Duffy visits in order to meditate. This description, like the presentation of Duffy's routine, increases by contrast our sense of the character's interior turmoil. By presenting Duffy's thoughts the teller reaches an extreme of style, after which he switches to another kind of narration for the next three stories. The switch that occurs between stories here is reminiscent of the change in "Eveline" when the narrator shifts his mode of narration in the final paragraph. And the change resembles the more extreme shifts of style in *A Portrait*. There is a strong irony at work in the style at the end of "A Painful Case" that makes the change appropriate. The longest, most vivid evocations of Duffy's interior voice present his growing realization that he has lost the voice he might have had. That realization silences even the voice he does possess. The interior voices of characters will be almost completely silent in the three stories that follow.

Momentarily, Duffy thinks he hears and feels Mrs. Sinico again: "At moments he seemed to feel her voice touch his ear, her hand touch his. He stood still to listen." This act of listening is the beginning of the end for Duffy's interior life, which has temporarily reached a pitch of sustained intensity before its demise. Besides presenting Duffy's thoughts as narrated and quoted monologue, the narrator renders that intensity in its final moments as the character's mind turning to metaphors in order to grasp its own plight. With these metaphors the narrator begins drawing away slightly from Duffy's perspective. Duffy thinks of himself twice in the penultimate paragraph as "outcast from life's feast." Then, as his interior colloquy stops, his perceptions begin to be largely metaphorical and symbolical. The "goods train" he sees in the distance looks "like a worm with a fiery head." He hears the "drone of the engine reiterating the syllables of her name." Once Duffy has associated the instrument of Mrs. Sinico's death with an infernal worm, which also suggests the decay of the body in the grave, the sound reminding him of her violent end displaces the interior voice that was his memory of Mrs. Sinico. After the locomotive moves out of hearing he can discover only a silence that is both external and internal: "He could not feel her near him in the darkness nor her voice touch his ear. He waited for some minutes listening. He could hear nothing: the night was perfectly silent. He listened again: perfectly silent. He felt that he was alone." As in the earlier climactic report of thought as if speech, this passage fuses inner and outer but with a reversal of implication, because the external silence replaces speech and indicates an interior silencing.

The earlier statement, "we are our own," resembles both gram-matically and rhythmically the story's final clause, "he was alone." But that final clause must be read differently from the earlier one. To end the story, the narrator chooses the mediation of psycho-narration rather than the more direct techniques of either quoted or narrated monologue he has used frequently in the preceding paragraphs. He moves sufficiently away from the character's perspective to provide another frame of reference. Because the statement occurs in the past tense rather than the present, we cannot read it as a gnomic expression or as audible speech, as we could the earlier remark. And it does not appear to indicate the character's clearly formulated interior speech. Instead, through psycho-narration, the narrator translates an unverbalized or partially verbalized feeling. Unlike the earlier statement, this one is singular, not plural. It applies specifically to the character *only* rather than to a couple or to the generality of humankind. There is no need now for the statement to be plural, or audible, or even verbalized: the character communes only with himself. The irony of the story's last sentence is vivid and startling: we can read it as an example and as the result of Duffy's "odd autobiographical habit" of mind, which ex-presses the essence of his habits.

Like the boy at the end of "Araby," Duffy reaches a state of mind that includes a self-conscious, negative judgment about himself. The boy's insight, however, concerns his connection to a social world populated by people similar to himself, no matter how unattractive he might find those people and the world he shares with them. In his antithetical perception, Duffy realizes with pain and guilt that his habitual decision to withdraw from intercourse of emotional and sex-ual kinds has resulted in his permanent isolation from others. The intensity of this realization overcomes the disdain that has always protected him from honest self-reflection. The boy's new insight pre-pares for the outward turn that occurs in "Eveline" with the shift to a third-person narration representing consciousness. Together with his cynical and pessimistic attitudes about the relations among people, Duffy's self-consciously perceived alienation provides an apt place in the volume for a shift to a narration in which consciousness seems hardly to be an element of character. In the conclusions of both "Eveline" and "A Painful Case," the style includes its own internal countermovement. In "Eveline," the concluding paragraph incorpo-rates as a kind of parenthesis a representation of the character's state of mind when the narrator inserts a simile into his otherwise external view. In "A Painful Case," although the inner view dominates the later portions of the story it turns into its own opposite when the character's thoughts become a judgment rendered by the character about his own status as an outsider. Like the boy of "Araby," Duffy has learned to see himself as others might see him but without the boy's possibility of developing a mature style of writing as compensatory intercourse for the communication he has destroyed.

Duffy's Last Supper: Food, Language, and the Failure of Integrative Processes in "A Painful Case"

Lindsey Tucker

Any discussion of James Joyce's "A Painful Case" comes up against three troublesome concerns. First, the story is one that Joyce considered one of the two weakest in *Dubliners*. Second, it contains a considerable amount of autobiographical detail lifted directly from the diary of his brother Stanislaus. Debate over whether this material was well assimilated has led to consideration of the third problem, the seemingly disparate clusters of images to be found in the story. These images—mainly religious and gastronomic—have not always served to clarify meaning, partly because the story is also concerned with the use of language and the dilemma of a would-be artist whose bifurcated personality and emotional impoverishment render him artistically sterile.

The presence of these different elements has produced a number of interesting analyses of the character of Duffy. Because of the numerous references to food and body functions, one critic has seen Duffy as a man of humors. Another has argued for Duffy as a compulsion neurotic, a latent homosexual with anal erotic tendencies. Still another critic, in a study of literary references used by Joyce, suggests that Duffy views himself as a Nietzschean superman and shares a number of affinities with his creator.

It may be possible, however, to better see these elements as related if we bear in mind Joyce's interest in the analogy of priest and artist, and if we recall his description of the artist in *A Portrait* as "a priest of

From *Irish Renaissance Annual IV*, edited by Zack Bowen. © 1983 by Associated University Presses, Inc. University of Delaware Press, 1983.

eternal imagination, transmuting the daily bread of experience into the radiant body of everliving life." The priest's performance of a ritual act is of importance here because it is through this act that the transformation, the creation of a new form, takes place. However, ritual is not just a projection of psychic images, but is also an exemplification of transformational processes that operate first on the alimentary level. As an analogue for the digestive processes—the ingestion of food, its transformation, the expulsion of waste—ritual contains the basic dynamics of emptying and filling.

Besides the relationship of food and body processes to ritual—a relationship which suggests the way consciousness interprets the world and integrates itself with it—language is also an integrative process linked to the dynamics of ingestion and expulsion. But the creation of meaning by language is also a transformation process whereby sensory material is ingested and then articulated as a new entity, from which qualitative meaning can be derived. As Erich Neumann says, "the symbolism of the alimentary uroboros extends linguistically to the highest levels of spiritual life. The notions of assimilation, digestion, rejection, or growth and giving birth are, like innumerable symbols of this zone, indispensable to any description of the process of creation and transformation" (*The Child,* trans. Ralph Manheim). To examine Duffy in the light of his eating habits, his anal erotic tendencies and his use of language as they become structured by ritual, may help to illumine the reasons for his failure as artist/priest and argue for the story as an artistically rendered piece.

As we have suggested, ritual is a dynamic process. Yet one of the most obvious qualities of Duffy's life is not its dynamic quality but its stasis. The stasis is much in evidence, especially in the early pages of the story. Here, emptying has become emptiness; filling has become retention. In fact, Duffy's very life is imaged in terms of emptiness. For example, the unused distillery beside which he lives, as well as the shallow river that runs by the culturally impoverished city, seem to be correlatives for his empty life, and reflect his inability to draw upon the unconscious for creative energy. Duffy's room is also characterized by emptiness. His walls are blank—image-less—and his bookshelves contain only two books that are mentioned specifically. One, the *Maynooth Catechism,* which contains only the summary of religious doctrine, emptied of essence, conveys this same sense of emptiness and loss of sacred transformational power. And the only rituals that Duffy takes part in—Christmas and the funerals of relatives—are not seen as having any sacred significance at all but have become empty conventions there only to "regulate the civic life." Duffy, we are told, lives a spiritual life, "without any communion with others," and obviously this word would seem to carry connotations of interaction, atonement and integration.

"Retention" is perhaps the best word to use in describing the stasis which characterizes Duffy's life, for everything about him suggests withholding and preservation. We are told that his face "carried the entire tale of his years," and he also has little expressive ability but does "compose in his mind."

Especially interesting in terms of this retentive faculty are Duffy's diet and eating habits. All foods mentioned here are in some way connected with preservatives. Lager beer is made by slow fermentation and long storage; his biscuits are derived from arrowroot, a tuberous plant, but are hard and dry; corned beef is preserved meat. The Bile Beans advertisement does not necessarily denote, as Warren Beck contends, "confusion of purposes," but is yet another comment on Duffy's retentive tendencies. For not only does it suggest a bogus, hence desacralized aid to process, but only the headline of the advertisement has been retained by Duffy and has been attached to his scraps of writings. The word "headline" not only characterizes the nature of his writing, which is fragmented, but it emphasizes the presence of polarities which are also important in the story.

Stasis, the stopping of process, leads us to a consideration of the fragmented nature of Duffy's consciousness, for this fragmentation is only a more intellectualized symptom of the same problem we can discern in his eating habits. Psychologists tell us that one characteristic of developing consciousness is its tendency to divide, to create oppositions. In Judeo-Christian culture, however, the polarities that are created caused a division between upper and lower body functions which have become rigid because the two were never seen as complements. This rigid separation once aided in the formation of the superego, but ultimately, the lower body pole has been rejected, and defecation, instead of being considered a creative act, has become associated with the expulsion of one's own evil.

In Duffy, who is a product of a Catholic background and of a priestly bent, no integration of such oppositions ever takes place. His aversion for the lower functions is seen in the way in which he lives "at a little distance from his body," and regards "his own acts with doubtful side-glances." He is also "a man ever alert to greet a redeeming instinct in others," yet we assume that for Duffy, a redeeming instinct is a contradiction in terms. He also expresses "a distaste for underhand ways," and his head is large, suggesting mental dominance over physical. His bookshelves are hierarchically arranged too; the *Maynooth Catechism,* a symbol of the superego, is on the top shelf, whereas the Wordsworth corpus, associated with emotion and even child consciousness, is kept on the bottom shelf.

In the area of language, Duffy evinces this same tendency to divide and repress. Writing materials are on his desk, but of written productions we have little evidence. His translation of Hauptmann is the first creative effort we hear of, but it seems more like the making of equivalents, than the making of a new form. Nor do his stage directions suggest more than a skeletal kind of expression.

For example, one of the objects on Duffy's desk is a sheaf of papers. The word "sheaf" means stalk, the portion of a plant severed from its roots and seed, containing neither the nourishing nor the reproductive functions, and seems an appropriate word for these scraps. They consist of occasional sentences "preserved" in a pile, and ironically announced by the Bile Beans headline. Duffy's preoccupation with sentence writing, also seems to suggest his bondage to a lower order of creation, merely sublimated into sentences but undergoing no further development. As sentences they remain components and fail to become whole, to take form.

This failure to take form, to become integrated, is suggested in other portions of the story as well. For example, Mrs. Sinico's response to Duffy consists of the metabolizing of his words. They are given form in her physical response, in the taking of his hand. But this offering of union between the intuitive and physical, the intellectual and spiritual, is denied by Duffy who has, in reality, denied the transformational power of his own words and their ability to become flesh. "Her interpretation of his words disillusioned him," he thinks, and we see Duffy's critical faculties remaining dominant and ultimately destructive as they succeed again in stopping process.

The kinds of sentences that Duffy creates are also worth noting. First, there are sentences that are never uttered or written, but instead retained. "We cannot give ourselves . . . we are our own," he thinks. Such supposed assertions of individualism, sometimes taken to be indications of a Nietzschean personality, seem suspect, however, because essentially Duffy desires to remain disembodied, to "ascend to an angelical stature," while the most potent force in his mind becomes his own "strange impersonal voice," also disembodied. Even his reading of the account of Mrs. Sinico's death is accomplished *in secreto,* with only the inaudible moving of his lips.

Perhaps nowhere is Duffy's self-division more in evidence than in the sentence he writes after he has broken off his relationship with Mrs. Sinico:

> "Love between man and man is impossible because there must not be sexual intercourse and friendship between man and woman is impossible because there must be sexual intercourse."

Here, connected by the conjunction "and," which serves to balance and set off the clauses against one another, are a number of significant oppositions:

love/friendship
man/man
man/woman
must be/must not be

The repeated words are interesting also: "because," "between," "sexual intercourse," and "is impossible" define the nature of his conflict. All the above are connectives or deal with states of connection, with the exception of "is impossible," which serves to deny these connections while it also acts as a counterbalance to the phrase "sexual intercourse." Beck notes that this sentence is taken verbatim from the diary of Stanislaus Joyce, and he feels that it is incongruous when attributed to Duffy because it is "saturated with strong sexuality." He argues that we do not see Duffy as having the sexual intensity suggested by this aphorism. Nevertheless, it is possible to argue that the intensity is there, but in a repressed or compulsive form.

The first clause would seem to have a suggestion of homosexuality about it, and obviously Duffy would fear such a union while he was at the same time attracted to it. But such a union might not be homosexual in nature so much as narcissistic. While narcissism is often seen as a condition of excessive self-love, it can also be viewed as a symptom of alienation. What Duffy's narcissism seems to suggest is a need for self-unification rather than the need for a homosexual union.

Duffy's fears become more evident in the second clause. Friendship with a woman means for Duffy a reconciliation with an opposite or alien energy. Because the female (in reality his own female side), is still experienced as an unknown, a mystery and a danger, he is unable to relate to a woman as a benign and positive transforming power. To do so he would have to penetrate her darkness, have intercourse (again in symbolic as well as in real terms), but subconsciously, intercourse remains to him a devouring and destructive idea.

The end of the story shows the reactivation of a ritual which, because it is a desacralized one, fails to effect integration. To begin with, Mrs. Sinico's death seems profane for a couple of reasons. First, it is a death by way of words. Second, by urging Duffy to "let his nature open to the full," Mrs. Sinico has invited him to bear a symbolic sacrificial wound, to accept his creative female nature. But Duffy, who temporarily is able to confess to her, to open himself at least partially, refuses this sacrifice.

But as he reads the account of her death, Duffy begins to undergo a kind of mortification. The passion of Christ, which begins with the Last Supper and ends with the crucifixion, is parodied in the last supper of Duffy. Duffy, who always "read the evening paper for dessert," is forced on this occasion to come to terms with the death of Mrs. Sinico. His reading of the account seems to produce two separate responses, both of which illustrate his divided nature. His first and truest response is physical, but he also attempts to respond to the news on a critical and intellectual level. He denounces the form of the article (his inclination is always to separate form from content), and he notes "threadbare phrases," inane expressions of sympathy, and "cautious words." Yet the intellectual play on form is being countered constantly by a strong physical response to content, and this physical response acts as a purge, causing an attack on his stomach and nerves. Again we see Duffy's repression of body concerns failing as his physical nature insists on manifesting itself, and his real reaction to the event becomes expressed in a number of body images, especially ones associated with anality:

> He saw the squalid tract of her vice, miserable and malodorous. His soul's companion! He thought of the hobbling wretches whom he had seen carrying cans and bottles to be filled by the barman. Just God, what an end! Evidently she had been unfit to live, without any strength of purpose, an easy prey to habits, one of the wrecks on which civilization has been reared. But that she could have sunk so low! Was it possible he had deceived himself so utterly about her? He

remembered her outburst of that night and interpreted it in a harsher sense than he had ever done.

The references to lower body functions, although sometimes disguised, are numerous here, as are references to emptying and filling. Duffy's desire is that Mrs. Sinico should assume all the evil and physicality of his life, purge him of his own physical nature, become his scapegoat. But his attempt fails, and Duffy enters a state of ritual initiation where a battle with himself takes on new force.

First he abandons his usual eating habits, and, forsaking his water and cabbage grease (sorry substitutes for wine and blood) he gets himself a drink. Then his memory of Mrs. Sinico begins to work. Basically, Duffy's memory seems to operate on a simple retentive level. Early in the story for example, he tries to "fix" Mrs. Sinico in his memory (109). But now, instead of acting to preserve, memory becomes a means of creating a new form. Because of Duffy's changed relationship to the content of the memory, the memory itself takes on a new form. As he relives his life with Mrs. Sinico, he creates for it a new meaning. He conceives of her in a different way. He feels her loneliness, and his entry into memory is a kind of union with her. In his walk through the park, he almost succeeds in making this memory physical. "At moments he seemed to feel her voice touch his ear, her hand touch his." But his awareness of his own withholding, life-denying nature precludes union, and from the crest of the hill, Duffy can only view from a distance the "venal and furtive loves" that do celebrate life below.

Duffy then sees himself an "outcast from life's feast"; yet this important ritual ingredient, the communal feast, symbol of reintegration, is denied him. Instead, he feels "his moral nature falling to pieces," and undergoes a kind of dismemberment. What Duffy never realizes is that he has become his own feast. But the sacrifice that should be a prelude to regeneration or new birth is here a futile one. Duffy has already allowed Mrs. Sinico to undertake the real sacrifice for him, and by causing the death/sacrifice of her—his creative half—he has in effect killed himself and has become his own scapegoat and bearer of his own evil.

The supreme irony is that by denying the physical, Duffy has remained a prisoner of it, locked in anal consciousness. The anal imagery of the last two paragraphs seems particularly important. The train, whose "laborious drone" reiterates the syllables of her name, is a "worm with a fiery head," phallic, but also anal. As the rhythm of the engine dies away, so too does Duffy's memory. "He began to doubt the reality of what memory told him," Joyce says, and Duffy's creation, his new form, has passed away like a poorly digested meal. In the end, Duffy is left with no sound, no words, no creation, in a darkness that does not symbolize mystery, but emptiness.

Thus it would seem that Joyce's interest in the consciousness of the artist, his ability—or inability—to create form, is one that gets serious and powerful treatment in "A Painful Case," and problems regarding authorial distance and the indiscriminate use of autobiographical detail diminish beside our awareness that for Joyce, art was an integrative process, sharing affinities with all other processes, psychic and physiological, and even being dependent upon them. While this concern may get more successful treatment in his later work, "A Painful Case" still remains an important and artistically rendered story.

Gabriel Conroy Sings for His Supper, or Love Refused ("The Dead")

Ross Chambers

> *Little Tom Tucker sang for his supper.*
> *What shall we give him? White bread and butter.*
> *How shall he cut it without a knife?*
> *How shall he marry without a wife?*

PARASITES

Gabriel and Michael are the messenger angels, charged the one with the Annunciation, the other with heralding the Day of Judgment. In "The Dead," Gabriel Conroy and Michael Furey figure in a story about messages, set at Epiphany time, and inviting consideration of its own status as message, that is, its relationship to noise.

It is a commonplace of communication theory that there is no message without "noise": since there must always be a channel of communication, there is also a degree of interference between the message's transmission and its reception. But, putting it another way, this means that noise is a *condition* of communication and less an accidental condition of disorder, perhaps, opposing the message's order, than the fundamental and primary ongoing circumstance of chaos against which the message labors to constitute itself. If so, to be in touch with "noise" is to be in touch, not with some accidental happenstance, but with something fundamental, and indeed a message in its own right.

We know that in certain circumstances, say, the ringing of the

From *Story and Situation: Narrative Seduction and the Power of Fiction.* © 1984 by the University of Minnesota. University of Minnesota Press, 1984.

telephone that interrupts the guests' conversation at the dinner table, noise *can* be a message in its own right. And my telephone conversation, when I answer the phone, becomes a message (or exchange of messages) against which the table talk now functions as "noise," just as the phone conversation is "noise" to the talk around the table. One message, therefore, can be noise to another, and that is why there may be rivalry between messages and a need to distinguish between them in terms, for example, of their quality, urgency, significance, or value. This is the issue raised in "The Dead" by the Misses Morkan's Twelfth Night party, with its music, speeches, dancing, laughter, and applause, for this social intercourse figures as noise against the background of which are received intimations of another sort, or epiphanies—manifestations that function in turn as cosmic noise interfering with the cozy world of the party.

In an extraordinary book by Michael Serres (*Le Parasite*), from which I have borrowed the example of the dinner conversation and the phone message, a case is made for relating communicational "noise," as the *parasite* in the channel (the French word *parasite* translates "interference" or "static"), to parasitism in its biological and social senses: the organism that lodges in the host's body and derives life from it (and whose presence may sometimes be vital to the health and well-being of the host) and the guest who eats at the host's table without reciprocating in kind (but without whose presence, perhaps, the party would not "go"). "Sans lui," says Serres of the latter, "le festin n'est qu'un repas froid."

> Le parasite est invité à table d'hôte. Il doit, en retour, égayer les convives de ses histoires et de ses ris. En toute exactitude, il échange de bons morceaux contre de bons mots, il paie son repas, il l'achète en monnaie de langue. C'est le plus vieux métier du monde.

Here is a description of a parasite that reads like a comment on the character of Gabriel Conroy, the person who, however uncomfortable and out of place he feels in the company of his two old aunts—"ignorant old women," as he thinks them—their niece and their guests, is regarded by them as indispensable to the success of their gathering and who willingly carves the goose, supplies an after-dinner speech carefully calculated to please, and in an awkward moment provides relief in the form of an anecdote. In the English idiom, he sings for his supper, exchanging words for hospitality: and since he has artistic

pretensions, as a school teacher with an awareness of the languages and
culture of the Continent and as a book reviewer for *The Daily Express*
(two other forms of parasitism), he can be seen as a figure of the artist
as parasite. I mean the artist who is nourished materially, but also
culturally and spiritually, by a society to which, in return, he gives
words that please and entertain, words without which the party would
not "go" and "le festin serait un repas froid"—the artist, then ("c'est le
plus vieux métier du monde"), who prostitutes himself. But singing
for one's supper is also a byword for exclusion, and the admonition to
"sing for your supper" rings sometimes like the Ant's rejection of the
Cicada, in La Fontaine:

> Vous chantiez? j'en suis fort aise:
> Et bien! dansez maintenant

—just so, the problem in "The Dead" will arise from the fact that
parasitism as social inclusion is incompatible with another form of
"parasitism" (as affinity with cosmic "noise") and, as such, amounts to
an exclusion from love. As in the nursery rhyme, singing for one's
supper poses Gabriel the problem of being married "without a wife."

Noise Within and Without

"It was always a great affair, the Misses Morkan's annual dance. . . .
For years and years it had gone off in splendid style as long as anyone
could remember"; that this should again be the case is the aunts' great
concern, and the secret of their reliance on Gabriel. However, their
soirée is readable, and in the context of *Dubliners* inescapably so, as a
figure of Irish society or, more accurately, of Dublin life. Gabriel, in
his speech, insists on the Irishness of the occasion and on the exem-
plary quality of the three ladies' hospitality:

> Of one thing, at least, I am sure. As long as this one roof
> shelters the good ladies aforesaid . . . the tradition of genu-
> ine warm-hearted courteous Irish hospitality, which our fore-
> fathers have handed down to us and which we in turn must
> hand down to our descendants, is still alive among us.
> A hearty murmur of assent ran around the table.

But there are, of course, many ironies here, and the culture being so
warmly praised by the speech maker speedily reveals significant deficiencies when one takes the party as a genuine reflection of it. The

absence of Miss Ivors, the militant nationalist ("It shot through Gabriel's mind that Miss Ivors was not there and that she had gone away discourteously") strikes a dissenting note amid the congeniality. And the living tradition of hospitality, as many readers have remarked, succeeds only partially in masking a pervasive sense of death, or at least of that moral "paralysis," the cultural "hemiplegia"—half-life or half-death—that is a central concern of *Dubliners*. For "tradition" it is easy to read "repetition," and to recall—thinking of Johnny the horse— that the Misses Morkan have been giving the same annual party, with the same guests, the same menu, the same entertainment, the same jokes and anecdotes and speeches, for "a good thirty years." "Never once had it fallen flat."

But the *danger* of its falling flat is always close to the consciousness of reader and characters alike, and the Misses Morkan and their guests (Gabriel foremost among them) work hard to ensure that everything goes off, as it should, "in splendid style." An awareness of the imminent death of the more aged participants (Aunt Julia and Mrs. Malins) is complemented by more subtle hints of the "last end" toward which all are proceeding, and if Gretta is thought on her arrival to be "perished" with cold, it is Gabriel's turn, at the end, to dwell on thoughts of mortality ("Soon, perhaps, he would be sitting in that same drawing-room, dressed in black. . . . Yes, yes: that would happen soon." The "funferal," as Joyceans enjoy saying, is akin to a "funeral." Meanwhile, the cultural chatter of the party reveals a society isolated in its own provincialism, and turning—again like Johnny the horse—in the circle of its own past experience, a milieu in which not only is Browning alien but the opera singers of the local past are deemed superior to those of a European present that includes Caruso. And the few dissident voices (Gabriel with his partiality to Continental "fads" like galoshes, Bartell D'Arcy with his awareness of foreign musical life, and Mary Jane, who would "give anything to hear Caruso sing") serve largely to point up the general complacency.

A gloomy feast, then, were it not for the effort being made by those present to enjoy themselves and—on the part of those who, like Gabriel, are not enjoying themselves—to make the party nevertheless "go," for the others, at the price of words and actions that are, from one angle, warm and well intentioned; from another, forced, mendacious, or hypocritical. The irony is patent in the words of the ritual song with which the guests salute their hosts:

For they are jolly gay fellows, [etc.]
Which nobody can deny.

Unless he tells a lie,
Unless he tells a lie.

The cohesiveness of the group ("the singers turned towards one another, as if in melodious conference . . . then, turning once more
towards their hostesses . . . ," is at its height here, but their harmony is
built, precisely, on a lie: the lie of their "jollity" and "gaiety," a lie
akin to that of the toastmaster who calls the Misses Morkan "the Three
Graces of the Dublin musical world" and wishes three "ignorant old
women" "health, wealth, long life, happiness and prosperity." Without such lies, the feast would indeed be a cold one.

Putting this another way, the party appears poised precariously
between the order of its harmony, warmth, and good feeling and the
disorder—the sense of a dying world—that constantly threatens it. In
similar fashion, music competes—as an expression of the festive mood—
with noise. But the music is formalized and contained within the
conventions of the well-programmed soirée. Aunt Julia sings her piece
in a voice of great purity: "To follow the voice, without looking at the
singer's face, was to feel and share the excitement of swift and secure
flight"; but the face bears a "haggard look" that foretells her death, and
the choice of her aria, "Arrayed for the Bridal," contrasts pathetically
and ludicrously with her spinsterhood and advanced age. As for Mary
Jane's party piece, "full of runs and difficult passages," it "has no
melody" for the listeners, who drift away bodily, or mentally (Gabriel
thinks of death, connoted by the engravings of Romeo and Juliet and
the little princes in the tower, and of the resentment he feels toward his
dead mother); and they return just in time to furnish the lie of their
acclamation. It is something of a relief, one feels in both cases, for the
listeners to be able to lapse into the noise making of applause (be it
genuine, as in Aunt Julia's case, or hypocritical, as in Mary Jane's); just
as it is, perhaps, in the case of the acclamation that follows the
rendition of "For they are jolly gay fellows" or the burst of "applause
and laughter" that greets Gabriel's sally about the Three Graces. Such
noise is a response to slight embarrassment. But it still has the quality
of expressing social cohesion and harmony, as does the dancing, where,
however, music borders more perilously still on disorder and dishar-
mony. It is while dancing the lancers that Miss Ivors "picks her crow"
with Gabriel; and in the preparatory hush preceding Gabriel's speech,

one hears the piano "playing a waltz tune and . . . the skirts sweeping against the drawing-room door" (for the young people have supped first). So, it is against a background of insistent disturbance that he must make himself heard throughout his address, the parasite's words of comfort being themselves accompanied by the parasitical presence of noise in the communicational situation.

The self-same sound of waltzing had greeted Gabriel on his arrival at the party: "He waited outside the drawing-room door until the waltz should finish, listening to the skirts that swept against it and the shuffling of feet"; and it accompanies the initial conversation between Gabriel and Gretta and their hostesses, itself punctuated by laughter (Gretta "broke out into a peal of laughter. . . . The two aunts laughed heartily too"). But noise, of course, characterizes the description of the whole party. The "clapping of hands" that signals the end of the waltz also accompanies Julia's announcement: "Here's Freddy" (a noisy entry that will be significantly repeated at a later point). Gabriel "recognized Freddy Malins' laugh. Then he went down the stairs noisily." Meanwhile, laughter and the excited clapping of hands accompanies Mr Browne's pleasantries and the organization of quadrilles, and when Gabriel reappears with Freddy, "he was laughing heartily in a high key at a story which he had been telling Gabriel on the stairs" (another anticipation of a significant later event). Soon Freddy is again exploding, in midnarration, "in a kink of high-pitched bronchitic laughter"—a first instance in the narrative of storytelling traversed by noise.

If the early stages of the party are thus interspersed with laughter and clapping, supper—announced by "the clatter of plates and knives"—is the occasion for considerable din: "There was a great deal of confusion and laughter and noise, the noise of orders and counter-orders, of knives and forks, of corks and glass-stoppers"; and the aunts refuse for a long time to settle, "toddling around the table, walking on each other's heels, getting in each other's way and giving each other unheeded orders." After a new "clatter of forks and spoons" accompanying dessert, the anticipatory lull preceding Gabriel's toast is "broken only by the noise of the wine and the unsettlings of chairs" while a few gentlemen pat the table, both as encouragement for the speaker and as "a signal for silence"; the speech itself being given, as has been noted, against the background of waltzing in the next room.

At departure time, laughter again breaks out (Mary Jane's, Aunt Kate's, Mr Browne's); and general merriment accompanies Gabriel's anecdote of Johnny the horse, the conclusion of which is greeted by renewed "peals of laughter" that are interrupted in turn by Freddy's "resounding knock at the hall door." As the guests enter their cab, there is "a great deal of confused talk." "Aunt Julia and Mary Jane helped the discussion from the doorstep with cross-directions and contradictions and abundance of laughter." Finally, the cab "rattle[s] off" "amid a chorus of laughter and adieus." The relative silence of the walk, and drive, to the hotel and of Gabriel's and Gretta's *coucher* forms a perceptible contrast with all this festive noise.

And festive it is, warm and expressive of social cohesion, whatever communication disorder it may introduce into the situation. But it is associated also with a long series of small incidents—ineptnesses, gaffes, maladroit behavior, all the "noise" of social intercourse—that are themselves suggestive of an underlying cultural disarray. I am not thinking so much of the major divisions and dissensions that center mainly on Gabriel and D'Arcy, the two artist figures: the contrast between Continental culture and Dublin parochialism, that between the anglicized East and the deeper, rural roots of West Ireland, whence Gretta comes, and which Miss Ivors reproaches Gabriel for betraying (to these we will return). It is more a matter of a series of uncomfortable moments. The aunts are at first worried because Gabriel is late; Freddy Malins, on the other hand, "always came late," but they are "dreadfully afraid that [he] may turn up screwed"—which proves to be the case (although this time he is only slightly tipsy). Gabriel's conversational failure with Lily, which draws a bitter retort, and his failure to make amends by a Christmas tip "discompose" him and crystallize his feelings of disquiet about the speech he has prepared: "Their grade of culture differed from his. He would only make himself ridiculous by quoting poetry to them which they could not understand. . . . His whole speech was a mistake from first to last"—this while he listens to the rustling and clacking and shuffling of the dancing within. The strained conversation about galoshes ("—O, on the Continent, murmured aunt Julia, nodding her head slowly. Gabriel knitted his brows") comes as a confirmation of this intuition.

But soon it is Mr Browne's turn to make three young ladies uncomfortable, by an innuendo in "a very low Dublin accent," and Mary Jane's to be embarrassed, "blushing and rolling up her music nervously" at the applause for her miscalculated showpiece (a lesson for Gabriel, this). Miss Ivors is a major source of social discomfort: not only does her accusation of "West Briton" grate on Gabriel so that he retorts "suddenly": "—O, to tell you the truth, I'm sick of my own country, sick of it!'', but she goads him into public conflict with his wife over the proposed vacation in Galway. Finally, she departs abruptly from the party before supper and on a most unconvincing excuse, leaving Mary Jane "puzzled" and Gabriel reflecting that "she had gone away discourteously." Another center of disruption is Mr D'Arcy, who at first refuses to sing, provoking Gretta's opinion that he is "full of conceit," then sings (apparently for his own pleasure or at least on his own whim) just as the guests are departing, and who, when reproached for having told a "great fib" in alleging a cold, responds "roughly" to poor Aunt Kate, leaving everyone "taken aback by his rude speech" and making it necessary for all to make embarrassed amends, the ones by displaying excessive solicitude for the slighted cold, the other by relating its history in circumstantial detail. (It is Mr D'Arcy, too, who, not realizing there is to be a toast, at first refuses wine.) But the gracious hostesses themselves are not exempt from social errors: Mary Jane's and Aunt Julia's musical performances are both, in different ways, poorly judged for the occasion; Aunt Kate gives "scandal" to Mr Browne, "who is of the other persuasion," by speaking ill of the Pope and working herself into an indecorous state of passion over her sister's eviction from the choir in favor of boy singers. It is Kate, too, who incautiously expresses irritation with Mr Browne ("He has been laid on here like the gas all during the Christmas") before adding sheepishly, "I hope to goodness he didn't hear me."

It is against noise, then, both in the literal sense and as a metaphor of social ineptitude, that Gabriel works to maintain order. In spite of his own social lapses and mental discomfort, his behavior stands out on at least two occasions for its smoothness and felicity. The after-dinner speech is, of course, one of them, and the other is his telling of the story of the "old gentleman" and his horse Johnny. At departure time, there is an awkward pause in the hall while Gretta is still upstairs (her slowness, one remembers, is the reason for the couple's symmetrically late arrival). Gabriel smoothes over the moment of waiting with an amusing anecdote concerning a treadmill horse that, when taken out for a ride, ends up obstinately circling the statue of King Billy (that is, William of Orange, the victor of the Boyne and hence a major oppressor of Ireland). Critics, who seem to have read the account of "noise" at the party as simple, realistic detail (for they do not discuss it), have also universally interpreted this story in terms of its content, as a comment on the containment and mechanical repetition that characterize Dublin's moral paralysis, that is, as a *mise en abyme de l'énoncé* (both with respect to "The Dead" and with respect to *Dubliners* as a whole). But the circumstances of the telling (the story as *mise en abyme de l'énonciation*) are also interesting and can begin to suggest to us something of the status of "The Dead" itself as a message.

In this respect, two factors are especially relevant. First, like the speech, the story is told in order to please: it is an example of Gabriel's parasitism at its most successful. His manner is droll, he is willing even to clown for the amusement of his hearers ("Everyone laughed, even Mrs Malins . . . Gabriel paced in a circle round the hall in his goloshes amid the laughter of the others")—an action that incidentally identifies him with the treadmill society the story is perceived to be about. This is Gabriel smoothing tension and producing group cohesion, as is his wont. But second, the story is told against a background of noise—a noise that manifests itself here in a way familiar to us, but also in a new way, for the sound that accompanies the initial awkward pause and the storytelling proper is slightly eerie: it is associated in the conversation with the cold, with a journey homeward, and by suggestion with death.

> —Someone is strumming at the piano, anyhow, said Gabriel.
> Mary Jane glanced at Gabriel and Mr Browne and said with
> a shiver:
> —It makes me feel cold to look at you two gentlemen
> muffled up like that. I wouldn't like to face your journey
> home at this hour.

The strumming is in preparation for D'Arcy's song, which means that the story will be accompanied by a sound of "distant music"—a noise that, associated as it is with the cold and a "homeward" journey, will come, as we will see, to constitute for Gabriel a message of deep significance, although it is here disregarded by the revelers in favor of the amusing anecdote.

A more familiar noise, which interrupts the concluding jollity, is associated with Freddy Malins, who manifests himself, not as facing a journey in the cold, but as coming back into the warmth of the house, out of the cold. There is a "resounding knock" that suggests some dramatic intervention from without, but it proves to be only the familiar drunkard, returning with a cab. Freddy, like Bartell D'Arcy, although in a different way, is something of an alter ego of Gabriel's: at the start, the two come upstairs together, as Freddy tells a story, and now, as Gabriel tells *his* story, their departures coincide. And it is not coincidental that Gabriel, with his concern for the smooth order of the party, would be told by the aunts to watch over Freddy throughout the evening, for the chronic drunkard with his high-pitched laugh stands as a major figure of festive disorder and misrule, everything, that is, that the aunts most fear and that Gabriel in his parasitic way, does his best to counteract. Freddy personifies noise: his voice, like that of his mother (who also stutters), has a "catch" in it that interferes with communication: "Freddy Malins bade the Misses Morkan good-evening in what seemed an off-hand fashion by reason of the habitual catch in his voice." It seems, then, that the two types of noise that accompany Gabriel's storytelling are polarized, as between the noise of festive warmth (Freddy) and something more uncanny, cold, and distant (D'Arcy); but Gabriel himself, whose message (the story of the horse) it is that defines both D'Arcy's hoarse ballad and Freddy's noisy knock at the door as interference, suggests in this refusal of both that they may well have something in common.

And indeed, Freddy's "catch" relates him to the scratch in the voice of the singer, who by reason of his cold is "as hoarse as a crow." The crow, in turn, is not only (as a vulgar version of the raven) a harbinger of death; it relates to yet another aspect of social dissension, the "crow" Miss Ivors wished to pluck with Gabriel—and hence, by contrast, to the goose, to the carving of which Gabriel was so relieved to turn on the departure of that intense lady. Gabriel in his role as entertainer and resident "goose" thus is seen to be quite deliberately masking the insistent presence of noise at the party, a noise that distributes itself along a kind of continuum that goes from the unruly disturbance of Freddy's disruptive presence to the distant sound of D'Arcy's singing, via the abruptness of Miss Ivors's intervention. And if D'Arcy's song relates to the cold outside and if Freddy is one who comes in to the party warmth, there is another sense again in which Miss Ivors—this time by her upsetting midparty departure—provides a mediating link between "inner" and "outer" noise.

It is important to see that the speech, too, functioning as it does to counter the "noise" of social ineptitude and discord so as to produce a mood of happy harmony, does so to the accompaniment of a form of party ("inner") noise that, in the reader's mind, comes gradually to be associated less with the merrymaking than with intimations from without, the cold external world where the snow is "general over Ireland." I am thinking of the rustling of skirts and shuffling of dancing feet, which relate in due course to the soft fall of snow (while the waltz tune in the other room provides its own "distant music"). Thus, running nervously over the heads of his speech as he stands outside the drawing-room door and waits to make his entrance, Gabriel is already aware of the music within and listens to "the skirts that swept against it and the shuffling of feet"—and this is the moment when he makes his decision to eliminate "noise" from the speech by omitting the Browning quotation as an impediment to communication. The speech proper is delivered to the same background of music and dancing: "The piano was playing a waltz tune and he could hear the skirts sweeping against the drawing-room door"—but here the repressed Browning snippet makes its inevitable return in the form of an allusion to the words ("thought-tormented music") that Gabriel had used to describe the poet's art: "But we are living in a sceptical, and, if I may use the phrase, a thought-tormented age." The little phrase not only tells us much about the form of art that Gabriel considers alien to this milieu, and about its affinity with noise; but his apology for it also conveys his sense that the phrase itself is out of place—functions as noise—in the cliché-ridden speech.

But throughout the evening, whenever Gabriel has begun to envision his speech, his mind has not only noted the noise from the other room, it has also swung to the world without, with its snowy but seductive alternative to the oppressive warmth of the party and its speechifying obligations:

> Gabriel's warm trembling fingers tapped the cold pane of the window. How cool it must be outside! How pleasant. . . ! The snow would be lying on the branches of the trees and forming a bright cap on the top of the Wellington Monument. How much more pleasant it would be there than at the supper-table!
>
> He ran over the headings of his speech.

and:

> The patting at once grew louder in encouragement and then ceased altogether. Gabriel leaned his ten trembling fingers on the tablecloth. . . . The piano was playing a waltz-tune and he could hear the skirts. . . . People, perhaps, were standing in the snow on the quay outside, gazing up at the lighted windows and listening to the waltz music. The air

was pure there. In the distance lay the park where the trees
were weighted with snow. The Wellington Monument wore
a gleaming cap of snow that flashed westward over the
white field of Fifteen Acres.

   He began:

—Ladies and Gentlemen.

Tappings and pattings of fingers, swishings of skirts and shufflings of
feet, remote and thought-tormented music, leading to . . . the snow.
This is not the place to rehearse the many complex and subtle readings
that the "symbol" of the snow has given rise to in "The Dead." The
association with death (and the West) is inescapable; but my purpose is
to suggest that the association with noise is both germane and firmly
written into the text and that, in contradistinction to the form of social
disorder that Gabriel combats in making his speech, the snow figures a
form of noise that encompasses social noise but transcends it and forms
an insistent alternative to his speech, that is, another message. In this
respect, snow relates, of course, to the figure of Michael Furey, Gabriel's West of Ireland alter ego out of the past, here evoked in an
anticipatory way both by the motif of "gazing up" (as we will learn
that Michael once gazed up, from the garden below, at Gretta's window) and by the association with the West. But later the reader will
realize also that it is the lost sound of Michael Furey's "gravel thrown
up against the window—that now lives on eerily—not only in the
pattings and tappings of the party, not only in Freddy's rat-a-tat-tat at
the door as he returns with the cab, but also (as Gabriel's final perceptions make clear) in the flutter of snow against the windowpane.

> A few light taps upon the pane made them turn to the
> window. It had begun to snow again. He watched sleepily
> the flakes, silver and dark, falling against the lamplight. The
> time had come for him to set out on his journey west-
> ward. . . . His soul swooned slowly as he *heard* the snow
> falling faintly through the universe and faintly falling, like
> the descent of their last end, upon all the living and the dead
> [my emphasis].

Here, then, the association with the dead Michael has become something more general, an association with the universal "last end," while
the snow appears as noise made visible and "falling faintly through the
universe"—a background of cosmic disorder, then, that has all the

evening through accompanied the party, with its own internal compo-
nent of social disorder. And although the party excludes this disorder
as best it can, it has been ever present at the windows, so that Gabriel's
tapping on the pane from the inside with his own nervous fingers
seems in retrospect to have been the sign of some response within him
to this message from without.

Gabriel's parasitic words are proof against social disorder, as we
have seen. But against the noise, the rival message—cosmic in its
reach—of death? Against grief (the noise-traversed narrative of Aunt
Kate, "crying and blowing her nose and telling him how Julia had
died"), Gabriel knows that his comfortable clichés are impotent. "He
would cast about in his mind for some words that might console her,
and would find only lame and useless ones. Yes, that would happen
soon." We must now investigate more closely Gabriel's relationship
to the message of cosmic disorder.

DISTANT MUSIC

Gabriel's storytelling and speech making spring from a deep and
good-hearted instinct: the desire to maintain social harmony in a situation in which it is patently threatened by disorder. But a strain of
negative judgment on social parasitism runs through the story, from
Lily's memorable definition of men as sexual parasites (that is, seducers), "The men that is now is only all palaver and what they can get
out of you," to Gabriel's own bitter self-evaluation at the end:

> A shameful consciousness of his own person assailed him.
> He saw himself as a ludicrous figure, acting as a pennyboy
> for his aunts, a nervous well-meaning sentimentalist, orating
> to vulgarians and idealising his own clownish lusts, the
> pitiable fatuous fellow he had caught a glimpse of in the
> mirror.

That one feels the latter judgment to be excessive is evidence of the
sympathy the story generates for what is warm and human in Gabriel;
but what forces general agreement with the thrust of his self-estimate
is, of course, the reader's understanding of the experience that pro-
vokes it in Gabriel, the "epiphany" of which he is distantly cognizant
but that finally excludes him, as Gretta excludes him from love. There
is a form of "parasitism" that is not directed *against* disorder but
expresses an alliance with the *source* of noise; and the story makes it

clear, on the one hand, that this is much the more significant form of artistic parasitism and, on the other, that, sensitive as the socially seductive Gabriel is to *its* seductions, he is inadequately equipped—emotionally and aesthetically—to respond to them.

For what was noise to Gabriel's storytelling proves soon to be a genuine act of communication, taking place between Bartell D'Arcy, the singer identified with the world of European art, and Gretta, with her origins in the West of Ireland (that is, the two characters who, apart from Gabriel himself, are least identified with Dublin); and of this act Gabriel can only be an intrigued spectator. D'Arcy, it will be recalled, is the man who *refused* to "sing for his supper," a social gaffe he now compounds by choosing to sing, without audience and as it were for his own pleasure, just as the guests are leaving, adding final insult to injury by being ungracious when reproached with this:

> —I have been at him all evening, said Miss O'Callaghan, and Mrs Conroy too and he told us he had a dreadful cold and couldn't sing.
> —O, Mr D'Arcy, said Aunt Kate, now that was a great fib to tell.
> —Can't you see that I'm as hoarse as a crow? said Mr D'Arcy roughly.
> He went into the pantry hastily and put on his overcoat.

His affinity with cosmic noise expresses itself first of all as social ineptitude, in direct contrast with Gabriel's smoothness.

But D'Arcy's cold is not just an excuse, it is quite real and it is associated, at least in Mary Jane's mind, with the snow, being the occasion of her key pronouncement: "I read this morning in the newspapers that it is general all over Ireland." And, partly as a result of his cold (which gives him something in common with Gretta, who is also so afflicted), his singing has qualities that distinguish him from the other characters. If his hoarseness recalls the "catch" in Freddy Malins's voice, D'Arcy is a singer whereas Freddy only produces laughter; and although his voice, conversely, is like Aunt Julia's in being a trained and "lovely" one, which "all Dublin is raving about," it differs precisely from hers (which is "strong and clear in tone") in that it is "made plaintive by distance and the singer's hoarseness," the performer seeming "uncertain both of his words and of his voice." Moreover, although D'Arcy shares Gabriel's taste for things Continental, he differs from the latter in his affection for Irish folk culture: the song "seemed to be in the old Irish tonality" and is identified in due course as a folk song from the West, "The Lass of Aughrim." Finally, the singer's art, combining noise and loveliness, the Continental and the deeply Irish, is an expression of grief: in this it contrasts by its genuineness both with Aunt Julia's inopportune "Arrayed for the Bridal" and with the lying chorus of "For They Are Jolly Gay Fellows." It contrasts, too, with the laughter-traversed storytelling, not only of Freddy but also of Gabriel. In short, dissonant as it is with the whole mood of the Dublin party, D'Arcy's singing is a manifestation of all that the party excludes. It is in this that it is clearly figures an artistic alternative to lenitive speechifying and jolly storytelling.

It comes, this music, from such a distance—social, cultural, and metaphysical—and the communication of its message is so tenuous that the listener has to strain to hear it. If the preparatory piano strumming is background noise to Gabriel's anecdote of the "old gentleman" and Johnny, the noise of joyous leave-taking interferes much more drastically with Gabriel's reception of the song:

> He could hear little save the noise of laughter and dispute on the front steps, a few chords sung on the piano and a few notes of a man's voice singing.
> He stood still in the gloom of the hall, trying to catch the air that the voice was singing.

And a moment later:

> The hall-door was closed; and Aunt Kate, Aunt Julia and Mary Jane came down the hall, still laughing. . . .
> Gabriel said nothing but pointed up the stairs towards where his wife was standing. Now that the hall-door was closed the voice and the piano could be heard more clearly.

Gabriel, then, grasps the music and its message only imperfectly. The person who truly *hears* it, thanks to her position closer to the source—although she, too, must concentrate with full attention—is his wife, the "country cute" Gretta from Galway, less well educated than he but more attuned to genuine Irish culture. *She* is illumined by it: "There was grace and mystery in her attitude as if she were a symbol of something."

> Gabriel watched his wife who did not join in the conversation. She was standing right under the dusty fanlight and the

> flame of the gas lit up the rich bronze of her hair which he
> had seen her drying at the fire a few days before. She was in
> the same attitude and seemed unaware of the talk about her.
> At last she turned towards them and Gabriel saw that there
> was colour in her cheeks and that her eyes were shining.

But *he,* who does not receive the direct impact of the message, can only wonder at its significance and imagine how, as an artist, he might render it.

> He asked himself what is a woman standing on the stairs in
> the shadow, listening to distant music, a symbol of. If he
> were a painter he would paint her, in that attitude. Her blue
> hat would show off the bronze of her hair against the
> darkness and the dark panels of her skirt would show off the
> light ones. *Distant Music* he would call the picture if he were
> a painter.

There is, then, a distance between him and the prime recipient of the already distant message, which not only increases the message's faintness but also alters the whole problematics of the situation: Gabriel is here less concerned with capturing and transmitting the message of D'Arcy's singing than with communicating, through the conventional techniques of art (symbolism and composition—the showing off of part against part), a sense of its impact on another. His concept of art has little to do with the noise-traversed music of the distant singer.

Yet it is this distance—not between him and D'Arcy but between him and Gretta—that the rest of the narrative, as the story of his aroused desire and its disappointment, now shows him attempting to traverse. Gabriel does not know it, but his relationship to Gretta and hers to the distant song map directly onto the love triangle, soon to come to light in the final embedded act of storytelling, involving Gabriel, Gretta, and the long-dead Michael Furey, who "had a very good voice" as she says and sang "The Lass of Aughrim" before dying for her. And his desire for Gretta's body, "musical and strange and perfumed," is a desire for conjunction with that place that is itself in direct communication with the music that comes from so far away. The distance to be traversed is in part a distance in time—the time separating the estranged present from the honeymoon period of his and Gretta's shared "secret life": her first letter to him in the heliotrope envelope; the ticket he slipped into her warm glove; the strange episode of the glassmaker, when they were together looking *in* from the cold, toward the warmth and noise of the furnace. And the arrival at the hotel goes give Gabriel a sense of having revived that period, of escaping from "their lives and duties" and running away "together with wild and radiant hearts to a new adventure."

But—of this Gabriel is less consciously aware—the distance to be traversed involves also a journey into death. Only the reader, perhaps, catches the connotations in the crossing of O'Connell Bridge, with its eerie encounter confirming the significance of the snow ("—I see a white man this time, said Gabriel") and the grimly ironic equivalence between the funereal, and noisy, cab ("The horse galloped along wearily under the murky, morning sky, dragging his old rattling box after his heels") and Gabriel's honeymoon memories ("galloping to catch the boat, galloping to their honeymoon"). So, too, in the dark and silent hotel, where the "soft thuds" of their feet, the sound of falling candle wax and the thumping of Gabriel's heart correspond to the faint sounds of the falling snow, recorded elsewhere, and where the porter with his light figures the psychopomp conducting the couple to their resting chamber (Gabriel here feels his soul stirring with life), the reader perceives something like an entry into the land of the dead. A "ghostly light" illumines the bedroom, and Gretta, turning from her mirrored reflection and walking "along the shaft of light towards him," is herself like a shade, coming to greet Gabriel and to accept him into that world.

From the past, Gabriel has retained the sense both of the power of words and of their inadequacy:

> In one letter that he had written to her then he had said: *Why is it that words like these seem to me so dull and cold? Is it because there is no word tender enough to be your name?*
>
> Like distant music these words that he had written years before were borne towards him from the past. He longed to be alone with her. When the other had gone away, when he and she were alone in their room in the hotel, then they would be alone together. He would call her softly:
> —Gretta!
> Perhaps she would not hear at once: she would be undressing. Then something in his voice would strike her. She would turn and look at him.

There is a word "tender enough," there is "something in the voice" that Gabriel is aware of "like distant music" and that would have the power of making accessible the object of his desire. Can he produce this word? As Gretta turns from the mirror, it is indeed in response to her husband's naming of her: "—Gretta!" But, for Gabriel, it is a moment of failure. "Her face looked so serious and weary that the words would not pass Gabriel's lips. No, it was not the moment yet." Gabriel's failure of nerve, in this whole episode with Gretta, is the sign of an artistic and indeed metaphysical inadequacy, a fatal lack of initiative, an impotency. There follows the "false" little conversation about the loan repaid by Freddy Malins, Gretta's kiss, and finally—"in an outburst of tears"—her confession: "O, I am thinking about that song, *The Lass of Aughrim*." Words are not the means of their coming together, of the satisfaction of Gabriel's desire: *his* words do not break down the distance between him and the recipient of the distant singing, so *her* words—noise-tormented like D'Arcy's song and like the tearful narrative of Aunt Kate, whom Gabriel will imagine "telling him how Julia died"—will be the measure of their separation.

When Gretta tells the tale of Michael Furey, she speaks in a voice "veiled and sad," a voice threatened each moment by tears ("She paused for a moment to get her voice under control"), a voice of grief. This, now, is the distant song communicating itself to Gabriel. But the words convey a message of exclusion, since the tale of Furey's selfless passion and simple devotion, the picture of him in the streaming rain outside the window, Gretta's confession: "I think he died for me" contrast so painfully with Gabriel's own emotional timidity and passionlessness, and with the self-image he now has as "pennyboy for his aunts." "Shy of intruding on her grief" (all of Gabriel's failure is in this phrase), he abandons all thought of possessing her and walks— once more—"to the window." Storytelling, we know, is frequently an act of seduction; but the point of Gretta's story has been, on the contrary, to mark an exclusion and ratify a distance: the communication it establishes concerns the impossibility of a communion.

As such, it confirms the situation already produced by D'Arcy's singing—a situation of exclusion that, one can now see, echoes redundantly throughout the text of "The Dead." "The Lass of Aughrim" is *mise en abyme de l'énoncé*: it is the story of a sexual rejection, and the words quoted in the text are those spoken by the lass as she stands, seduced and abandoned, in the rain—like Michael in Gretta's grandmother's garden—outside the Lord's tower. And Gabriel's exclusion from intercourse with Gretta, like his exclusion from the rapt communication between D'Arcy and Gretta through his song, repeats his sense of exclusion from the cold, snowy world that is the ultimate object of his desire—an exclusion that, by virtue of his own self-willed inclusion in the warm world of the Misses Morkan's party, he has brought on himself but that, so many times in the course of the evening, has brought him, in thought or deed, "to the window." If the "noise" that so insistently traverses the jolliness and warmth of the party is itself a message, and a message of great attractiveness to both Gabriel and Gretta, then that message is nevertheless a message about the necessity, the inevitability of exile for those who heed it. Gretta is an exile—from the West, from the past, from the love of Michael, from all the "distant music"—just as Gabriel is himself an exile from her love.

It is only in sleep, with the cessation of desire, that Gabriel achieves some sensation of union, or near union, with the world of cosmic disorder that fires his longing. Turning "unresentfully" from Gretta, he contemplates the hotel room, with its disorder reflecting the "riot" of his recent emotions and recalling the evening's merrymaking; and his mind then adverts to the alternative pole, to the universality of death. "One by one they were all fast becoming shades." Drifting into sleep, he seems to approach, although not quite to attain, the world of death. His tears of pity—for the aging Gretta, for himself—fuse now with a vision of Michael "standing under a dripping tree." "Other forms were near. His soul had approached that region where dwell the vast hosts of the dead. He was conscious of, but could not apprehend, their wayward and flickering existence." As his identity fades and the world dissolves, the falling of the snow, "general all over Ireland," represents the dissolving, impalpable universe, its solidity gone; and as his soul swoons, he continues to hear the soft noise of its faint descent. Gabriel has left the world of order and is now at the very threshold of an alluring new world, of disorder perhaps, but of disorder soft and inviting. "The time had come for his journey westward"—westward into death, no doubt, but also to the source of the allurement he had felt when watching the effect of D'Arcy's singing on Gretta—westward toward Michael's snow-clad burial ground, but farther westward still to where the snow falls into the "dark mutinous Shannon waves." Westward into the heart of the storm. The universe of meteorological disorder has become *the* world, for Gabriel, and it is time for his journey. But the journey has yet to be made.

"The Dead," it seems, poses a clear alternative in the choice between the artistic parasitism exemplified by Gabriel's speech making and the affinity with noise embodied in D'Arcy's song. But the narrative models it offers are, in fact, three in number; and they constitute a group of options to all of which the text can be seen, in some sense and to some degree, to conform. All are ways of relating to cosmic noise. Gabriel as speech maker and storyteller relates negatively to such noise; Gretta as storyteller, like D'Arcy the singer, mediates noise as a message; Gabriel, finally, as spectator of Gretta's rapt listening and rejected lover, mediates the sense of cosmic noise in a more remote and distanced fashion.

In light of the contrast with the epiphanic episodes, Gabriel's speechifying and storytelling cannot be seen as a positive model of the story's own narrative situation. Yet there is an uncomfortable sense in which, like the other stories in *Dubliners,* "The Dead" is parasitic on the Dublin society from which it takes nourishment (subject matter) and to which it gives, in return, words (information). The words, to be sure, are bitter, ironic, and scarifying, as opposed to Gabriel's flattery and clowning; but in "The Dead," at least, they are not without a redeeming, positive side. We know that, writing this story some time later than the others in the collection, Joyce was anxious to correct its uniformly negative tone, in particular by acknowledging the warmth of "Irish hospitality." In a sense, then, Gabriel's speech does function as a direct model of the story's own narrative situation; and it is, of course, ironic that such artistic parasitism should be pointed up precisely apropos of the national gift for hospitality. It is ironic, too, and significant, that—precisely because it was written later, after the collection was completed, and from a changed angle of vision—the story functions, within the structure of *Dubliners,* as a parasitic and disordering element. Not only does it, in thematic terms, introduce an unwonted positive note, but the story interrupts also the chronological ordering, in terms of the stages of life, that controls the other stories as a group. We might do well, instead of struggling to make this story cohere with the rest, to see that its function is not to cohere but to introduce *in extremis* a new note and a new message. In this it is not unlike Mr D'Arcy's belated singing at the party, both *of* the party and *not* of it, a disturbance to its harmony.

For it is clear that the story's major commitment is to noise, to noise as social disturbance and cosmic disorder, the two functions performed by D'Arcy's singing. Noise is everywhere present in "The Dead," like the laughter that convulses Freddy in midstory or the tears that traverse Gretta's narrative; but unlike these models—unlike Aunt

Kate's grief-stricken story, as imagined by Gabriel, also, and unlike D'Arcy's hoarse song—the story speaks *of* noise without itself constituting noise. It does not speak noise or speak noisily; its narrative technique is, on the contrary, entirely coherent and indeed conventional—it is the technique of Joyce the Irish Maupassant or Zola. So, we learn from it about noise without actually hearing in its own narrative "voice" the noise with which it is concerned. This is because the story is told, broadly speaking (the opening pages are focused through Lily), from Gabriel's viewpoint, and it is Gabriel's distance from the phenomenon of noise that the reader is made to share. It is not accidental that Gabriel's model for dealing aesthetically with the epiphany of D'Arcy and Gretta is painting—an art combining realistic portrayal (the woman, her clothing, her attitude) with symbolic intent (conveyed in the title), but one from which, most obviously and inevitably, the single most important missing element is D'Arcy's voice itself. His hoarse song cannot be embodied in words that conform to the aesthetic to which Joyce subscribes in his story, an aesthetic in which there is no place, except as subject matter, for communicational noise.

Does such an aesthetic exist? Is there a form of literary art that would place the reader, with respect to the song, not in Gabriel's distant position but in that of Gretta, the more direct and immediate recipient? This would be an art speaking not the conventional language of storytelling that excludes us from "noise," but a discourse of noise, conveying directly and with immediate impact the message of disorder and death, an art destructive of order yet "melodic" in its own way and in its own terms. With hindsight, and mindful of the connection between the combination of deep Irishness and European sophistication in the epiphany of Gretta and D'Arcy and the self-same combination in the character, biography, aesthetic formation, and artistic practice of James Joyce himself, it is easy to see that the art for which D'Arcy is the model, the art of verbal noise and snowy disorder, will eventually be embodied in the author's future writing, in modernist, "writerly" texts such as *Ulysses* and *Finnegans Wake*. Like Gabriel drifting into sleep, "The Dead" has brought us to a point at which "readerly" narrative is at the threshold of its crossing over into the unleashed energy, the disorder, and the soft, alluring beauty of the "writerly" snowstorm.

A bird is missing, then, from the aviary of (edible) fowl in "The Dead." If Gabriel is a "brown goose" (brown being the color, in *Dubliners,* of the city's paralysis), he is destined to "eat crow," less at the hands of Miss Ivors (whose connection with the West is neverthe-less highly relevant) than at those of D'Arcy, who has the crow of death in his throat. But the model for the story is neither the goose nor the crow, but something in between, for it is a swan song. It is the swan song of *Dubliners* as D'Arcy's song is the swan song of the party, but as such it constitutes a farewell to its own aesthetic and the announce-ment of an aesthetic yet to be discovered. The swan, as Socrates pointed out, is not mourning its own death but, knowing beforehand "the good things of the other world," acts as prophet of a better future "in the presence of the god." One may imagine its song a little like D'Arcy's, melodious and beautiful but with a hint of "crow," or like the narrative of "The Dead," couched in the aesthetic language of "this side" but traversed by many hints of the beauty and allure of the "other side." Joyce's story, strangely, speaks from out of an aesthetic space, a situation that is, as yet, absent, using discourse that belongs, by its own reckoning, to an already outmoded past.

No more fitting exemplification could be found than this of the "spectral" character of narrative situation in texts, always of the text and constructed by its discourse, but always dependent on a construing in the future, from outside of the text and independently of it. That is why the reader must be both seduced by the text, with all its alluring requirements of "understanding" or love, and yet maintained in his or her own freedom, refused by the text, as Gabriel is excluded by Gretta, the better to constitute that always future situation indispensable to its life. If, as narrative texts approach the "writerly"—"Un cœur simple," "The Figure in the Carpet," "The Dead"—the reading situation they construct tends progressively toward greater and greater openness, none of them neglects the seduction of the reader, whose involvement is ensured by mimetic duplicity, coerced spectatorhood, or here, exac-erbated desire. The reader's participation in the perspective and emo-tions of Gabriel does not go without a certain distancing from Gabriel, whose deficiencies, inadequacies, and "unresentfulness"—human as they are—are difficult to share. As readers of "The Dead," we share the perspective of exclusion—from the love of Gretta, from the source of cosmic noise—that is his, but our desire does not abate so easily as we follow him in his slow swoon toward death; for our perspective is also that of Michael Furey, who does not take rejection by Gretta quite so tamely, and whose desire, far from abating, becomes strengthened as it merges with a desire for death. Gabriel, lying beside Gretta, can easily picture "that image of her lover's eyes when he had told her that he did not wish to live," and he knows that such tenacity as Michael's, as opposed to his own "shy[ness] of intruding on her grief," is the sign of genuine passion. "He had never felt like that himself towards any woman but he knew that such a feeling must be love."

The loving reader, whose desire remains alive even as Gabriel drifts into the death of sleep, is the shadowy figure—"the form of a young man standing under a dripping tree"—that the text projects, as the ghost of Michael, into its own future. "Other forms were near. . . . He was conscious of, but could not apprehend, their wayward and flickering identity." These "hosts of the dead" with whom, as his own identity "fade[s] out," Gabriel gradually merges occupy the situation from which the story asks to be read, the perspective that Gabriel's own perspective will eventually rejoin, but only when he has completed the journey on which he is as yet only setting out. Not the unloving living but the dead, the loving dead, whose messages reach the world of the living as tempest and noise, are the readership the story craves but cannot define. The dead of its title are of the future, not the past.

"The Boarding House" Seen as a Tale of Misdirection

Fritz Senn

The following views are offered as supplementary angles from which we might profitably talk about Joyce's "The Boarding House." Some of its features are those of a love story; we find all the conventional trappings: a young girl and a not so young man; they are brought together by circumstance and opportunity; there is the promise of a marriage in the near future, except that things are not quite as they ought to be; things are out of place. The ruling passion is practically absent, and what is present seems to be awry. The couple, it takes little imagination to discern, is mismatched, united by direct and implicit forces and by scheming. What is in evidence is the trapping. "The Boarding House" gains much of its poignancy by being set off against a backdrop of sweet, comforting fiction of the "Matcham's Masterstroke" type. It is a love story of wrong turnings.

Its misdirection involves readers by leaving them largely out of the main events. We realize how we are cut off from the crucial events, both of them; we are detained by moments in between; the actions are off stage. We are never informed what actually happened between Mr. Doran and Polly Mooney. We learn about the enticing beginning of the affair but not its completion. We may guess, of course, and we may think we know enough. Still, the overall narrative agency and all three main characters are in harmonious collusion in withholding the facts from us. We are not even told anything concrete about the interview between mother and daughter of the night before in which,

From *James Joyce Quarterly* 23, no. 4 (1986). © 1986 by the University of Tulsa.

we read, "a clean breast" had been made "of it"; nor about Mr. Doran's confession. Nothing specific is passed on to us. Whenever we come close to that recent "sin" as the cause of it all, the narrative drifts into vagueness, generalities, "his delirium . . ." or "secret amiable memories . . . a revery"; we are not let into the secret of "every ridiculous detail." The ellipsis after "delirium," Joyce's, needs to be filled, and filled it will be, by a few readers with more certainty than the facts may warrant. The sin is one for which "only one reparation" can be made (there is tacit agreement on this between Mrs. Mooney and Mr. Doran's priest, who both use the word independently, which in turn tells us that the case is a standard one, not unique), but still small enough to allow of being "magnified" by a priest. The one chief witness and victim remembers an exchange of "reluctant good-nights" on the third landing. All things known considered, Mr. Doran might have to pay for much less than what we almost automatically charge him with: this would make the reparation more cruel, less contingent on deed than on mere social attitudes, "honour," or reputation, hearsay and gossip. Anyway, we were not there, and this gap is paralleled by the one in the present, the decisive interview when Mrs. Mooney will be "hav[ing] the matter out with Mr. Doran." There is no need for us to be on the spot (nor is Polly's presence required). The issue has been predetermined by a determined woman in full charge, and by Mr. Doran's known "discomfiture." Like a general before a battle, Mrs. Mooney has marshalled her forces, her arguments, even their phrasing. We may well stay with Polly and the vaguest of her memories, waiting, alone. We can fill *this* narrative vacuum easily, though we were somewhere else, apart.

The story's technique is one of "elsewhereness." There is a synoptic exposition, and then the story splits up into three distinct parts and two locations; each of the three characters is seen mainly in isolation. Separation is indeed a theme. Mrs. Mooney married her father's foreman and, when things went wrong, "got a separation"; "they lived apart." Mr. Mooney, in the process, is cut off from family, occupation and even identity. When he—"a disreputable sheriff's man"—turns up, plaintively, in his daughter's office, he is not even given a name. Mrs. Mooney, for the rest of the story, is seen engaged in compensatory matchmaking, a venture which takes a good deal of manipulation. Joining together and putting asunder are correlated activities. Mrs. Mooney is "able to keep things to herself"; she knows when to intervene. She removes her daughter from home to an office, or back home from the office. The height of social life in the boarding house on Sunday nights is "a reunion" (and the rise of social tone is matched in that choice word, "reunion") in Mrs. Mooney's "front drawing-room." Even language seems to put on its Sunday dress and to "oblige," as do the *"artistes."* (Note what difference the French spelling and the French aura make: *"artistes,"* not to be confused with "artists," come from somewhere else, and not the most reputable place, which shows in other contexts—"a likely *artiste,"* a few lines before.) If a misplaced "free allusion" is made, "the reunion" can be "almost broken up." A more lasting reunion is now being engineered for the two lovers, but we also learn that this is a scheme for achieving what "some mothers she knew" could not do—"get their daughters off their hands." Minuscule separation ("pieces of broken bread") and joinings ("the broken bread collected") can be aligned coincidentally, almost in the same breath; the same sentence has Mrs. Mooney beginning "to reconstruct" the interview of last night—taking apart and putting together.

Mrs. Mooney is successful in her strategies of keeping "her own counsel," watching, or throwing people together, or separating them. For this latter activity her emblematic tool is well chosen. A butcher's daughter and once a butcher's wife, "she dealt with moral problems as a cleaver deals with meat." It was a cleaver also that her husband used when "he went for" her. It was after that that she "got a separation." It is odd and may be superfluous to reflect that the first woman ever created was made out of the first man's flesh—"bone of my bone, flesh of my flesh"—and the injunction was that he "shall cleave unto his wife" (Gen. 2:23–24): but that is a wholly different "cleaving"; following a misdirected association, we are in the wrong shop.

There are other, related, contrasts. A sense of fixation, being stuck, enclosed, is pitted against the freedom of movement. Once the action gets under way, we are confined within the boarding house. People may move from room to room, but nobody is ever described as leaving. Mrs. Mooney reflects that a man "can go his ways," but she takes good care that Mr. Doran cannot. For him to "run away" is an inconceivable alternative. Instinct urges him to "remain free" and "not to marry." As he follows Mrs. Mooney's summons downstairs, he longs "to ascend through the roof and fly away to another country," his own impracticable variant of a general inept desire for escape in *Dubliners*. It is then that he passes Jack Mooney coming up from the pantry, and it happens "on the last *flight* of stairs" (italics throughout are part of the comment, not the quotation). At precisely the moment when no turning away is possible, no reversal towards freedom, bulldog-faced and thick-armed Jack Mooney regards the lover "from the door of the *return*room." Everybody seems to be static in a room for most of the time. Among the trumps in Mrs. Mooney's hand is the threat that publicity would mean for Mr. Doran "the loss of his *sit*." So we find him sitting "helplessly" in his room. When he leaves it, it is not to get away from Mrs. Mooney; he will have to walk straight into her parlor.

There is plenty of movement in the story, but it tends to go the wrong direction. Mr. Mooney "began to go to the devil"—not an ideal destination; he "ran"—but "headlong into debt"; "he went for his wife." Then, relegated, he is "obliged to enlist" in an office, where he sits "waiting to be put on a job." When he shows up at Polly's place, things go wrong again, and she has to be ordered home, out of harm's way, there to be given "the run of the young men." A *run* might be a free, unhampered moving about; but the playground is narrowly defined. In fact Polly's "run" is resumed, in different words, in an echoing phrase: "Polly, of course, flirted with the young men," where unobtrusively, "run" has become part of a trite idiom for the naturally expected: "of course" implies that the run, course (*cursus*), of events is foreseeable, can be taken into cunning account. To "flirt" once designated a movement (of jerking and darting); it is now limited to the arena of courting with its own tacit rules. "Polly, *of course,* flirted" is in gentle tune with the governing determinism, a reliable fatality that Mrs. Mooney knows how to work to her own advantage. Her husband once was "sure to break out" (from the pledge into renewed drinking); her son is "sure to be on to a good thing" (and to lend some threat or muscular help, when necessary). In this world a likely lodger can be expected to toe the line; "a force" pushes him "downstairs step by step." The combined forces may include "the weight of social opinion" or publicity, which "would mean the loss of his sit." So Mrs. Mooney can be sure "she would win." Running the whole show, "a determined woman" (as the second sentence in the story states emphatically), she is resolute, active, but in turn also determined by her nature and her environment, perpetuating her own failures. Things take their course, occasionally with some skillful prompting, and the run may turn out to be a dead end, without a "loophole."

Most of the running, then, is in an undesired direction. There was a hitch in Mrs. Mooney's married life; her plans miscarried, so she now masterminds her daughter's fate. Mr. Doran would rather turn somewhere else, fly through the roof, than face his prospective mother-in-law, but he obeys. It is a short step from whatever he actually "had done" to being "done for." Even his smallest actions go amiss; he has a hard time doing anything right. He is fumbling, passive, conative: "He had made two attempts to shave but his hand had been so unsteady that he had been obliged to desist." We notice how the men in Mrs. Mooney's environment generally "oblige" or "are obliged." Mr. Doran can hardly see and could never "brazen it out." He is being sent for, summoned as to court: "she wished to speak with him" is a command that will be phrased, "the missus wanted to see him." In yet another, almost deadly mechanical, near-repetition towards the end, Mrs. Mooney speaks for him and calls her daughter: "Mr Doran wants to speak to you." Language allows for this usage; "wanted" is circumstantially appropriate. We know and she knows what Mr. Doran really wants; her public voicing of the intention that silent Mr. Doran cannot utter himself is a supreme example of muted, ironic misdirection.

It is misguided and unwise for a butcher to buy bad meat or to fight his wife "in the presence of customers"; for a young girl to go to "relight her candle" in a boarder's room; for a boarder to abuse the "hospitality" or to take advantage of a girl. It may also be unwise to force two people into lifelong cohabitation.

Even trivial matters are not quite right, somehow displaced. Sunday worshippers are on their way to George's Church, right outside the window. It is the wrong church (Protestant), the wrong time. Mrs. Mooney will "catch short twelve at Marlborough Street." This one is the Catholic and prestigious Pro-Cathedral. (If we are not familiar with Dublin usage and envisage, for a puzzled moment, a train in some railway station, then the wording has misdirected us.) One may pick the wrong social key, the unsuitable expression, making a "free allusion." Polly's brother, who resents such breaches of decorum, may himself deviate into "soldiers' obscenities": it is all a question of when and where and who. Polly's song (through which she is introduced to the reader), with its rhymes of "sham" with "am," takes us two different ways, towards appearance or towards a reality beneath it. She appears both as a "naughty girl" in a music-hall sort of role, and then again as someone of "youth and inexperience." And what are we to make of a paradoxical joining like "in her wise innocence"? Polly "had a habit of glancing upwards when she spoke with anyone"—she is looking somewhere else—that "made her look like a little perverse madonna." A "perverse" madonna is one who is turned the wrong way. Etymologically, but not culturally, "madonna" is the same as "Madam." The Italian and the French variants both go back to a Latin (*mea*) *domina*, which perfectly suits Mrs. Mooney who rules on high and knows how to put a religious front on a meretricious calculation, combining both roles with ease.

The perverse madonna with her candle in search of light guides Mr. Doran ultimately into a "delirium." A *delirium* originally meant a going out of one's furrow (Latin *lira*); or to draw a furrow awry, a going off the rail, another wrong turning, one that has serious results.

Reading "The Boarding House" amounts to a process of *redirection* (or, if you prefer, an interpretative "reparation"). We interpret—let us hope, not all in the same direction—what we are told. We translate such matter-of-fact assertions as "she was an outraged mother" from a truthful lament to a strategic social weapon. As it happens, "outrage" derives from *ultra*:beyond; it suggests going far in a certain direction, going beyond bounds. In the redirection of reading we may take up Mrs. Mooney's "He had simply taken advantage of Polly's youth and inexperience" and match it—and in particular the beautifully comprehensive *"simply"*—with the complex ritual of allurement that fills more than half a page in Mr. Doran's reminiscences, with candle, perfume, caresses, slippers, timidity, and opportunity. ("Advantage" has to do with "advance," going forward, taking decisive steps; and for all we are told the advances were not Mr. Doran's.) He himself, in worried contemplation of the affair, translates the allegations Mrs. Mooney will no doubt repeat to him into his own, equally subjective, parallactic, terse version: "he was being had" (passive, of course). In some sense, "The Boarding House" puts several discordant, incomplete presentations of the affair against each other (including Polly's own dreaming version). The affair itself, in the center, remains unverbalized.

Misdirection may affect the wording, the syntax, especially when uncomfortable issues are at stake: "There had been no open complicity between mother and daughter, no open understanding *but*." Pause a moment and wonder what, after "no open complicity . . . no open understanding," this *but* might lead to. A few lines before, a similar construction was linked by the same conjunction: "Polly, of course, flirted with the young men but Mrs Mooney . . . knew that the young men were only passing the time." So we continue: "but, though people in the house began to talk of the affair, still Mrs Mooney did not intervene." The sentence takes an unexpected, vacuous, turn, leaving us dangling, as though the sentence, and Mrs. Mooney's meditations behind it, had not dared to face whatever development, or "complicity," was to follow.

It is worthwhile inspecting the meaning of a notion like frankness: "she had been frank in her questions and Polly had been frank in her answers," as frank and symmetrical a statement as one could wish to see. The frankness has been duplicated, but it is contradicted when we stumble across four "awkwards" in close succession. The most elaborate sentence in the whole story, hurriedly unpunctuated, as though to get it over as painlessly as possible, turns awkwardness into a psychological and syntactical actuality:

> Both had been somewhat awkward, of course. She had been made awkward by her not wishing to receive the news in too cavalier a fashion or to seem to have connived and Polly had been made awkward not merely because allusions of that kind always made her awkward but also because she did not wish it to be thought that in her wise innocence she had divined the intention behind her mother's tolerance.

These are the circling movements of evasion. Embarrassment has become paraphrase (a cautious "speaking beside" the point). For once even Mrs. Mooney is caught in a passive construction: "she had been made awkward." The frankness alleged earlier surfaces now as "allusions of that kind"; allusions, by definition, are not "frank." Latin co-nivere meant to close one's eyes so as not to have to notice; the whole long-winded sentence connives in this. We can also reinterpret what is claimed to be "tolerance": a strategic ambush. To be "awkward" could not apply to an inelegance like "by her not wishing to receive," but it once meant to go in the direction of "awk," and "awk" was the wrong way, or back foremost. That is what the sentence windingly seems to do, turn on its heels, as though to act out its original as well as its present meanings. The fourfold "awkward" is right: "The Boarding House" is a story of awkwardness.

Apart from that one interview, however, Mrs. Mooney is quite self-assured, knows which way to turn. She is in command, sure of victory. "She governed her house cunningly and firmly." She dispatches her husband, her daughter, the maid where she wants them. Hers are the transitive, active verbs: "she had married her father's foreman," "opened a butcher's shop," "got a separation"; "had taken what remained of her money"; "made Mary collect the crusts"; "counted all her cards." She turned her husband out of the house, leaving him uprooted. She sent "her daughter to be a typist"; but there her displaced father intervened and made a nuisance of himself. The husband's removal somehow interfered with her daughter's positioning, and the two maneuvers backfired: so things, for all her crafty management of affairs, *were* awkward after all The present enterprise too is a success that we see as highly qualified and costly, and we naturally tend to extrapolate.

Joyce has in fact provided extratextual continuation into another book. In *Ulysses* the misdirection is carried further, in hyperbolic exaggeration. The boarding house has become a "kip" (*Finnegans Wake* takes it as far as "boardelhouse"); Polly a down-and-out exhibitionist "without a stitch on her, exposing her person, open to all comers" or a "sleepwalking bitch." In the retelling Jack Mooney's silent glare has become an articulated threat: "Told him if he didn't patch up the pot, Jesus, he'd kick the shite out of him." Dublin gossip has been at work on the "details . . . invented by some" and magnified them out of hand. Predictably, however, Mr. Doran has been progressing in the direction we imagined; he has followed in the traces of Mr. Mooney: on his annual bend, he is already drunk in mid-afternoon, unpopular among his companions, and saying the wrong things in the wrong place, further discomfited.

His "discomfiture" that we witness is both a perplexity and a defeat, but also what the term contains: a making up (Latin *conficere*), yet one that has gone in an unwanted direction: *dis*; a falling apart, a joining and a separation. It is like the engineering of a match and, at the same time, "going to the devil," rolled into one.

The general displacement extends to tiny touches. "The Boarding House" displays most of the ingredients of the happy-ending tale, including "caresses . . . blood glowed warmly . . . perfumed skin . . . kiss . . . the touch of her hand," physical prerequisites of love. It also features a heart, just one, and a heart that seems to behave according to romantic precedent: "He felt his heart leap warmly." This sounds comforting: a heart leaps (remember Wordsworth), and does so "warmly," until: "He felt his heart leap warmly in his throat." This is not where we expect a heart to leap; it has been transferred incongruously and subjectively. This dislocation can be matched with a later passage in which Mr. Doran remembers Jack Mooney shouting at a music-hall *artiste* who had referred "freely" to Polly at one of the reunions, that "he'd bloody well put his teeth down his throat, so he would." The throat may be a suitable, characteristic part of Mr. Doran's anatomy at this turning point in his life, a telling synecdoche, but in the multiple misdirection and general discomfiture of "The Boarding House," the throat has become a place where one's heart might encounter one's teeth. Only a butcher with determination, and a cleaver, could make this happen.

"Ivy Day in the Committee Room": The Use and Abuse of Parnell

Thomas B. O'Grady

In the "Nestor" episode of *Ulysses,* Stephen Dedalus recalls a phrase from William Blake's note for *A Vision of the Last Judgment*: like Blake, Stephen believes that "Vision or Imagination is a Representation of what Externally Exists. Really & Unchangeably. Fable or Allegory is formed by the Daughter's of Memory." An untypically self-conscious Dubliner, Stephen tells Mr. Deasy: "History . . . is a nightmare from which I am trying to awake"; but "memory" perpetuates the "nightmare," both for Stephen and for all Irishmen. "Forgetfulness is the property of all action," Friedrich Nietzsche asserts in *The Use and Abuse of History,* and it is, in fact, the inability of Irishmen to achieve "the capacity of feeling 'unhistorically' " that James Joyce recognizes as the ultimate source of Ireland's political "paralysis." For although as Mr. Henchy claims in "Ivy Day in the Committee Room," "Parnell . . . is dead," like Milton's Lycidas, who "is not dead / Sunk though he be beneath the watery floor," Parnell lives—"Fabled by the daughters of memory."

Ideally, according to Nietzsche, "The knowledge of the past is desired only for the service of the future and the present, not to weaken the present or undermine a living future"; however, "we must know the right time to forget as well as the right time to remember." In "Ivy Day in the Committee Room," Joyce portrays how "The historical sense makes its servants passive and retrospective." Through

From *Eire-Ireland: A Journal of Irish Studies* 21, no. 2 (1986). © 1986 by *Eire-Ireland,* St. Paul, Minnesota.

the attitudes toward Charles Stewart Parnell manifested in the political sector of Dublin life, Joyce presents the effects of an "excess of history," by which "life becomes maimed and degenerate." In fulfilling his intention to write "a chapter of the moral history of my country," Joyce adopts a version of what Nietzsche terms a "critical" attitude toward history: "He . . . bring[s] the past to the bar of judgment, interrogate[s] it remorselessly, and finally condemn[s] it." Or more precisely, Joyce portrays how the popular views of the past, and specifically of Parnell, function not "as a means to life," but as a deterrent to life. Thus, the *double entente* of "One grief—the memory of Parnell," the final verse of Joe Hynes's poem which concludes "Ivy Day in the Committee Room," renders ironic Hynes's intended patriotism, as it is in fact this "degree of . . . 'historical sense,' that injures and finally destroys the living thing, be it a man, or a people or a system of culture."

October 6, the day on which the story is set—the anniversary of Parnell's death—is a "short day . . . grown dark," "dismal and cold out of doors"—appropriately so, as this is Joyce's portrayal of and commentary on the political decadence of post-Parnell Ireland. But the principal symbolic manifestations of the memory of Parnell in "Ivy Day in the Committee Room" are found in the description of Richard J. Tierney's Committee Room (suggestive of Committee Room Fifteen at Westminster, the site of Parnell's treacherous leadership defeat in 1890). Lit by only a weak fire at first, and then by candles, the room fluctuates between "darkness" and "fire," "shadow" and "light." Throughout the story, the darkness is obviously symbolic of the condition of Irish politics without Parnell; the brief glimpses of light reflect only the past glory of Parnell. The strongest symbolic expression of the dark/light motif is that of Mat O'Connor burning one of Tierney's business cards: "Mr O' Connor tore a strip off the card and, lighting it, lit his cigarette. As he did so the flame lit up a leaf of dark glossy ivy in the lapel of his coat." Ivy, the evergreen symbol of the dead Parnell, provides the only glimmer of light in this political world of Dublin where one such as Tierney, a Poor Law Guardian—that is, an administrator of the Poor Law Amendment Act of 1834, which often forced the Irish poor to leave their own parishes in search of work—may run as a candidate in the Dublin Municipal elections on the ticket of the Nationalist party, a remnant of Parnell's party of the 1880s. In fact, when the room is finally candlelit, the decadence of Irish politics is suddenly revealed: "a denuded room came into view and the fire lost all its cheerful color" as the candles lit up the walls of the room, "bare except for a copy of an election address," Tierney's hypocritical manifesto. Frederick C. Stern proposes, indeed, that the candles which light the room are, appropriately, like the candles which the boy in "The Sisters" believes "must be set at the head of a corpse."

Marvin Magalaner and Richard M. Kain suggest, furthermore, that the darkness/light motif in "Ivy Day" is a representation of political Dublin as Hell. Some of the dialogue certainly substantiates this interpretation, as Tierney is referred to as a "mean little shoeboy of hell" and Crofton is greeted with "talk of the devil" and "blast your soul." But perhaps most expressive of the Hell imagery's significance is Joe Hynes's greeting to O'Connor and old Jack: "What are you doing here in the dark? said Mr Hynes, advancing into the light of the fire." His question has literal implications, of course, as the room really is dimly lit; and it has figurative implications with reference to the political ideals of Tierney's supporters; but it also has symbolic implications in its anticipation of Father Arnall's sermon on Hell in *A Portrait of the Artist as a Young Man*: "the fire of hell, while retaining the intensity of its heat, burns eternally in darkness." That is, the energy of Irish politics is either directionless or misdirected.

But perhaps the most important symbolic meaning which can be adduced from the fire in "Ivy Day in the Committee Room" is that which refers to the Phoenix. The story begins with old Jack raking the cinders together and ends up with Joe Hynes's declaration that Parnell's "spirit may / Rise, like the Phoenix from the flames, / When breaks the dawning of the day, / The day that brings us freedom's reign." Joyce does not simply borrow Egyptian myth of the Phoenix and impose it on the story; rather, there actually existed in Ireland a rumor that Parnell had not died and that he would indeed return to lead Ireland to independence. But the ironic intention behind Joyce's use of the Phoenix myth is obvious as, of course, Parnell is dead, and so is the one-time glory of Irish politics.

There is, however, a double irony involved in Joyce's use of the Phoenix myth, as though Parnell is indeed dead, the *memory* of Parnell pervades, as a living force, the minds of the cross section of Dublin society which gathers in Tierney's Committee Room. The range of feelings toward Parnell experienced by these representative Dubliners can be correlated with two of the three ways in which, according to Nietzsche, "History is necessary, to the living man":

> If the man who will produce something great has need of
> the past, he makes himself its master by means of monu-
> mental history; the man who can rest content with the
> traditional and venerable uses the past as an "antiquarian
> historian."

But it is the "critical" attitude which informs the whole of "Ivy Day in
the Committee Room," as this attitude is in fact a reaction against the
"monumental" and the "antiquarian" attitudes which the individual
characters in the story manifest, as "only he whose heart is oppressed
by an instant need and who will cast off the burden at any price feels
the want of 'critical history,' the history that judges and condemns."
As Nietzsche points out, "Each of the three kinds of history will
flourish only in one ground and climate"; implicit in Joyce's structur-
ing of the story is his belief that Ireland in the years immediately
following Parnell's death must forget the past and "Hold to the now,
the here, through which all future plunges to the past."

Joyce's description of Gabriel Conroy at the end of "The Dead"
indeed applies with equal poignancy to each of the main characters in
"Ivy Day in the Committee Room":

> His soul had approached that region where dwell the vast
> hosts of the dead. He was conscious of, but could not
> apprehend, their wayward and flickering existence. His own
> identity was fading into a gray impalpable world: the solid
> world itself which these dead had one time reared and lived
> in was dissolving and dwindling.

Mat O'Connor, for example, "a grey-haired young man, whose face
was disfigured by many blotches and pimples," is old before his time.
Because he has not learned "to live, above all, and only use history in
the service of the life that he has learned to live," he suffers from what
Nietzsche calls "the premature grayness of our present youth." O'Connor is a Parnellite, with his ivy leaf in his lapel, but he despairs of the
present and the future. He has compromised his principles by working
for the hypocritical Tierney, though "he spent a great part of the day
sitting by the fire in the Committee Room." O'Connor sits pathetically
before the fire from which he hopes that the Phoenix/Parnell might
arise.

In a related way, old Jack represents the old generation of Parnellites
that has been displaced by a society of reprobates like his son: "I done

what I could for him, and there he goes boozing about . . . What's the world coming to when sons speaks that way of their father?" Reminded of the days of Parnell, old Jack remarks, "Musha, God be with them times! . . . There was some life in it then." Like Mat O'Connor, old Jack holds, in effect, an "antiquarian" view of the past: recalling the time of Parnell lends "the simple emotions of pleasure and content . . . to the drab, rough, even painful circumstances of a nation's or individual's life." But as Nietzsche points out, this antiquarian history "degenerates from the moment that it no longer gives a soul and inspiration to the fresh life of the present." Both Mat O'Connor and old Jack find reflection on the past much more comforting than confrontation with the present. Antiquarian history "only understands how to preserve life, not to create it . . . Thus it hinders the mighty impulse to a new deed and paralyzes the doer."

It is obvious that both Mat O'Connor and old Jack work less than wholeheartedly for Tierney, and even then just for the money involved; in fact, it is this strict work-for-pay attitude which is the common denominator among Tierney's canvassers. In the days of Parnell, a man would volunteer for the cause, for the ideal; but now money is the only motivator: "How does he expect us to work for him if he won't stump up?" Money is the only incentive, it seems, for working for "Tricky Dicky Tierney" with "those little pig's eyes," who "only wants to get some job or other." Although they recall Parnell fondly, neither Mat O'Connor nor old Jack has hope of seeing his ideal fulfilled. So they feel no compunction about working for the corrupt Tierney, who "first saw the light"—obviously not even the dying light of the Phoenix/Parnell fire—in his father's Sunday morning bootlegging.

Mr. Henchy's attitude is particularly mercenary and, not coincidentally, anti-Parnellite. Ironically, his name can be read as a diminutive of "henchman"—faithful follower. That, he certainly is not: he condemns and slanders his boss, Tierney; he accuses Joe Hynes of being "a man from the other camp. He's a spy of Colgan's"; he puns on the misfortunes of Father Keon—"I think he's travelling on his own account"; and he declares unequivocally, "Parnell . . . is dead." Henchy clearly typifies the contemporary political hack in his hypocritical selfish manner. From the moment he enters the Committee Room, his words and his actions betray his true character:

—Sit down here, Mr Henchy, said the old man, offering him his chair.

> —O, don't stir, Jack, don't stir, said Mr Henchy.
> He nodded curtly to Mr Hynes and sat down on the
> chair which the old man had vacated.

Taking old Jack's chair, Henchy symbolically replaces the old ways which Jack both longs for and represents.

Furthermore, Henchy accuses Hynes of being just "a stroke above" "these hillsiders and fenians" who "are in the pay of the Castle"—that is, who are spies for the British. But he considers the possibility of running for city office himself, even as he acknowledges the corruption, the nepotism, and the favoritism inherent in contemporary politics; his malapropism, "in all my vermin" for "in all my ermine" (referring to the mayor's robes), is especially poignant as he considers who would be his private secretary and his chaplain: the impotent Mat O'Connor and the defrocked Father Keon. Moreover, Henchy's references to the treacherous Major Sirr, "that'd sell his country for fourpence—ay—and go down on his bended knees and thank the Almighty Christ he had a country to sell," is particularly applicable, ironically, to his own case. Just as Sirr, an Irish major in the British army, betrayed and arrested the leaders of the Irish Rebellion in 1798, so does Henchy betray the principles of Parnell in welcoming the proposed visit to Dublin of King Edward VII of England. Henchy's mercenary nature is evident: "The King's coming here will mean an influx of money into this country." The fact that the King's visit represents an endorsement of England's oppressive political domination of Ireland is not considered by Henchy.

Nor does he wish to consider "the analogy between the two cases" of Parnell and King Edward. The treatment of Parnell, condemned as an adulterer and betrayed by his followers (his "henchman"), does not present, for Henchy, a precedent for an Irish attitude toward the King, himself an adulterer; for the King is not a sinner, "He's a jolly, fine, decent fellow, if you ask me, and no damn nonsense about him":

> —Let bygones be bygones, said Mr Henchy. I admire the
> man personally. He's just an ordinary knockabout like you
> and me. He's fond of his glass of grog and he's a bit of a
> rake, perhaps, and he's a good sportsman. Damn it, can't
> we Irish play fair?

Henchy, with his mercenary double standards, his selfish ambitions, and his narrow-minded sense of justice, is typical of the Irishman who would like to destroy the memory of Parnell merely to assuage his own afflicted conscience. Symbolically, Henchy "snuffled vigorously and spat so copiously that he nearly put out the fire which uttered a hissing protest."

In his denial of Parnell, however, Henchy does not succeed in awakening from the "nightmare of history" in which old Jack and Mat O'Connor are also caught; rather, his obsession with trying to forget Parnell is his "Agenbite of inwit," his "remorse of conscience," and as such is simply a different sort of "antiquarian" history, as he attempts to create merely another version of the memory of Parnell. But his version suffers from the same limitations as old Jack and Mat O'Connor's:

> The antiquarian sense of a man, a city, or a nation has always a very limited field. Many things are not noticed at all; the others are seen in isolation, as through a microscope. There is no measure: equal importance is given to everything, and therefore too much to anything. For the things of the past are never viewed in their true perspective or receive their just value; but value and perspective change with the individual or the nation that is looking back on its past.
>
> (Nietzsche, *The Use and Abuse of History*)

Three relatively minor characters help to round out the cross section of society which Joyce presents in "Ivy Day in the Committee Room," and help to comment further on the disintegration of the political and the moral values of that society. Father Keon, "a person resembling a poor clergyman or a poor actor," represents the role of the priest in Irish society and politics: "it was impossible to say whether he wore a clergyman's collar or a layman's." As Yeats says of the Parnell case, "The Bishops and the Party / That tragic story made": it was the preaching of politics from the altar which ultimately ensured Parnell's downfall, and Father Keon, while an extreme example, is obviously representative of the too secular Irish priest. He is looking for Tierney's agent not for a religious purpose, but for "a little business matter." That Father Keon is a "black sheep," a priest relieved of his duties, is particularly appropriate, for as Mr. Casey in *A Portrait of the Artist* claims: "We go to the house of God . . . in all humility to pray to our Maker and not to hear election addresses." Yet the priests continue to be a powerful force in Irish politics, as Henchy's canvassing tactics suggest: "I mentioned Father Burke's name. I think it'll be all right."

Lyons and Crofton are two more of Tierney's canvassers. Although apparently one of those who condemned Parnell at the time of
his divorce scandal, Lyons is at least consistent in that he also condemns Edward VII. In doing so, however, he creates merely one more
version of the memory of Parnell, as he recollects only Parnell's
immoral conduct—at the expense of the dead leader's political integrity. Despite being a strong Nationalist, Lyons reveals his political
blindness in his loyal support of Tierney. Like Dante O'Riordan in *A
Portrait of the Artist,* who calls Parnell "A traitor to his country! . . . A
traitor, an adulterer!", Lyons fails to consider the irrelevance of Parnell's moral conduct to his political goals. Thus, his version of the
memory of Parnell is just as invalid as any version which would
"monumentalize" Parnell, which would perceive him in a positive
light for inspiration; for Lyons's memory of Parnell has weaknesses
similar to those which Nietzsche recognizes in "monumental history":
it "will never be able to have complete truth; it will always bring
together things that are incompatible and generalize them into compat-
ibility, will always weaken the differences of motive and occasion."

Lyons's association with Crofton is further evidence that his view
of Parnell has only limited validity; for, again like the "monumental"
view, it tends to "depict effects at the expense of causes." Crofton is a
Conservative (Unionist) who, "when the Conservatives had withdrawn their man . . . , choosing the lesser of two evils [the Nationalists
or the Fenians], he had been engaged to work for Tierney." Because of
his supposedly superior political preferences, "he considered his companions beneath him," and the best that he can say about Parnell is that
"he was a gentleman." Crofton's involvement with the Nationalist
Party implies the deterioration of the Nationalist ideal which Parnell
had made seem so attainable.

The only self-redeeming character in the story is Joe Hynes. In
contrast with O'Connor and all the others, he is, "a tall slender young
man"—young despite the fact that ten years have passed since Parnell's
death, and Hynes had been a supporter even then, as Henchy acknowledges: "There's one of them, anyhow, . . . that didn't renege him."
Now a supporter of Colgan, the Fenian candidate, Hynes endorses the
working-man, unlike Tierney and his followers, who seek only personal gain:

—The working-man, said Mr. Hynes, gets all kicks and no
halfpence. But it's labour produces everything. The working-

man is not looking for fat jobs for his sons and nephews and cousins. The working-man is not going to drag the honour of Dublin in the mud to please a German monarch.

But Hyne's most significant admission of his political stance is his poem, "*The Death of Parnell*: 6th October, 1891." This poem, so typical of those published at the time of Parnell's death in such newspapers as *United Ireland*, functions in several ways in the story. Not only is it an accurate example of the popular literary treatment of the Parnell story, but it also reflects on and illuminates the rest of "Ivy Day in the Committee Room." As a part of the Parnellite literary tradition, the poem contains references to "Our Uncrowned King"; to poetic "Erin"; to "coward hounds"; to Ireland's noble "statemen, bards, and warriors" and to her "heroes of the past"; and, of course, to the Phoenix. But hidden among these conventional phrases and references are a number of subtle allusions to Hyne's audience: they are clearly a "fell gang / Of modern hypocrites" with "coward caitiff hands"; their potential for "treachery" is unquestionable; they, in effect, "befoul and smear th' exalted name / Of one who spurned them in his pride." The "fawning priests—no friends of his" are represented, of course, by Father Keon. And the references to the "pyre" and to the Phoenix are obviously consistent with the symbolic significance of the atmosphere in the Committee Room.

But the image which best reflects Joyce's own attitude toward the betrayal of Parnell is that of betrayal "with a kiss." This Judas image is one which Joyce refers to ironically, in his essay "Home Rule Comes of Age," as Irish altruism: "They have given proof of their altruism only in 1891, when they sold their leader, Parnell, to the pharasaical conscience of the English Dissenters without exacting the thirty pieces of silver." Henchy refers to Major Sirr in terms which echo Judas's betrayal of Christ; then Henchy himself is seen as a Judas willing to compromise, for "capital," the integrity of his country; and all except Hynes are in the Committee Room, ultimately, in the hopes of getting paid for canvassing for a political candidate whom they neither like nor trust.

The only verbal acknowledgment which Hynes's poem receives is from Crofton, the Conservative, who "said that it was a very fine piece of writing." Actually it is not; but it is sincere—the only sincere expression in this story of post-Parnell Ireland. But it is also with Hynes's sincerity that Joyce's "critical" view of history takes exception.

Although for a purpose contrary to Lyons's, Hynes too "monumental-
izes" Parnell—in this case as a model to emulate. In evoking Parnell,
Hynes implies that "the great thing existed and was therefore possible,
and so may be possible again." In Joyce's 1902 review of William
Rooney's *Poems and Ballads,* however, he writes of patriotic poems like
Hynes's:

> They were written, it seems, for papers and societies week
> after week, and they bear witness to some desperate and
> weary energy. But they have no spiritual and living energy,
> because they come from one in whom the spirit is in a
> manner dead, or at least in its own hell, a weary and foolish
> spirit, speaking of redemption and revenge, blaspheming
> against tyrants, and going forth, full of tears and curses,
> upon its infernal labours.

Joyce continues in his view, warning of "those big words which make
us so unhappy," "those big words" which Stephen Dedalus fears—
words like "Patriotism."

Hynes's intended patriotism fails, however, for the very reason
that "Monumental history lives by false analogy; it entices the brave to
rashness, and the enthusiastic to fanaticism by its tempting compari-
sons." Ironically, though, even such an unhealthy response is not
elicited from Hynes's audience. "We all respect him now that he's dead
and gone," says Mat O'Connor; but it is in fact this comfortable
"respect" for Parnell which is the "paralysing" element in Irish politics, as this contemplation of Parnell releases the individuals from any
sense of concern for contemporary political integrity. As Joyce notes
shortly after the death of Fenian leader John O'Leary, "the Irish, even
though they break the hearts of those who sacrifice their lives for their
native land, never fail to show great response for the dead."

Several times in *Ulysses,* Stephen ponders the "actuality of the
possible as possible" in Aristotelian terms which "define movement
(*kinesis*) as the fulfillment of a *potentiality* qua *potentiality*" (*Natural
Science*). Parnell's presence in Irish memory can be considered with the
same implications which Stephen attaches to Pyrrhus and Caesar:

> They are not to be thought away. Time has branded them
> and fettered they are lodged in the room of the infinite
> possibilities they have ousted. But can those have been pos-
> sible seeing that they never were? Or was that only possible
> which came to pass?

Parnell "lives" in the Irish imagination because of "what might have been: possibilities of the possible as possible." Joyce recognizes, however, that the desired *kinetic* effect of the memory of Parnell on contemporary Irish politics cannot be fulfilled, that "it is clear that motion may be predicated of a thing only while the thing is actually functioning in the manner explained, and not before or after." Thus "the memory of Parnell," even as Joe Hynes evokes it, actually produces an effect of Aristotelian *stasis,* of "paralysis." The existence of the Dubliners gathered in the Committee Room is merely "an imperfect tense that never becomes a present . . . [:] 'being' is merely a continual 'has been,' a thing that lives by denying and destroying and contradicting itself."

"He is dead. Our Uncrowned King is dead," Joy Hynes laments; and in "Ivy Day in the Committee Room" Joyce implies Stephen's assertion of *A Portrait of the Artist*—that Ireland must "Let the dead bury the dead." Otherwise, as Nietzsche warns and as Joyce portrays, the dead will "bury the—living."

Narration under a Blindfold: Reading Joyce's "Clay"

Margot Norris

James Joyce's "Clay" is a "deceptively" simple little story by design: its narrative self-deception attempts, and fails, to mislead the reader. But as a special case of the blind leading the blind (in a spirit of blindman's buff suited to the centrality of children's games in the story), "Clay" also offers the multiple insights that come with the restoration of sight: it allows us to see the blind spots in Maria's story and to see ourselves as their cause, if not their instrument. Joyce displays a surprising technical maturity in this early work, whose object is, I believe, to dramatize the powerful workings of desire in human discourse and human lives. The perfect protagonist for this purpose is indeed the "old maid": a figure who seems to lack every-thing and therefore embodies total desire, a desire for the recognition and prestige that would let a poor old woman without family, wealth, or social standing maintain her human status in paralytic Dublin and that would let her story be credited by those who hear it. "Clay" will attempt to mislead the reader, and it fails when we become deaf, as it were, and start seeing.

The narrational manipulations produce a particular style, intended to impress the narratee, that has sometimes ensnared the critic as well. Let me demonstrate. In developing an allegory of Maria as "the Poor Old Woman or Ireland herself," William York Tindall writes, "Shop-keepers condescend to her; and when a British colonel is polite to her on

From *PMLA* 102, no. 2 (March 1987). ©1987 by the Modern Language Association of America.

the tram, she loses her cake." A British colonel? The narration tells us only that "Maria thought he was a colonel-looking gentleman and she reflected how much more polite he was than the young men who simply stared straight before them." Tindall has risen to the narrative bait and has swallowed Maria's efforts to inflate the bumptious attentions of a garrulous old drunk into the courtly devoirs of a gentleman of rank from the ruling class. Unimportant in itself, this small mistake is symptomatic of a larger impulse in the story's critical history, which, curiously, mirrors Maria's quest. Readers and critics can no more accept the possibility of Maria's insignificance than can Maria herself. The impulse behind the critical treatments of "Clay," with their heavy emphasis on allegorizing Maria in some form—as either Witch or Blessed Virgin, for example—is therefore a collusive response to the story's rhetorical aim of aggrandizing Maria. This allegorizing tendency extends beyond the boundaries of the story to what Attridge and Ferrer call the "transcendentalist" approach to Joyce's fiction, which they trace back to T. S. Eliot's influence. Motivated by the need to save modern fiction from charges of triviality, vulgarity, and nihilism, critics assimilate literary works to larger symbolic orders and traditionally sanctioned value systems.

This need to create significance out of pointlessness also shapes the readings that most of my students bring to my classes: specifically, that the meaning of the story depends on interpreting the "clay" as "death"—as though this insight produced some sort of punch line, some sort of illumination that makes sense of an otherwise meaningless joke. Death is, course, a privileged figure in medieval allegory, and, in this interpretation, Maria's failure to perceive its prophetic beckoning through the symbols of the game makes her—all evidence of her sincere Catholic piety to the contrary—a vain and foolish *Jedermann*. But the reading of "clay" as "death" is anomalous within the context of the story, for even if Hallow Eve is the night the dead walk abroad in folk tradition, the thought of death is conspicuously absent both from the narration and from its representation of Maria's thoughts. When Joyce does want a story read through a tropology of "death" (as in "The Dead" or a "Hades"), he weaves a complex texture of incident and allusion to guide us to his meaning.

A different way of reading "Clay" derives from the interpretive backfire that reveals a lack of significance operating at the heart of the desire for it. The critics' need to capitalize Maria, to transform her negative attributes into positive symbols—from poor old woman into

Poor Old Woman, from witchlike into Witch, from virginal into Blessed Virgin—betray how little esteem the ungarnished old maid can muster. Joyce, I argue, does not promote the old maid to metaphoric status as much as he explores her need, and her strategies, for promoting herself. These strategies are narrational and rhetorical, as "Clay" becomes her defense against her interiorization of all the derision and contempt that has been her traditional portion. To the extent the defense fails, the reader is implicated, functioning as a critical actor in the story. The social consequences and psychological costs of feeling oneself designated as insignificant become a repressive force that splits all the discursive elements of the story in two: the story's subject, its narrative mode, and its reader. Maria divides into two versions of herself (into admirable and pathetic, bourgeois and proletarian, Lady Bountiful and victim), the narration is split into testimonial and exposé, prattle and pantomime, empty language and expressive silence, and the reader is split into gullible narratee and cynical critic, flattered ear and penetrating gaze, consumer of realism and dupe of naturalism. This fractured discourse of "Clay" is produced by the interplay between the two senses of *significance* working through the text: *significance* as an experience of psychological importance or ontological prestige, and *significance* as the linguistic or semiological meaning produced by modes of signification. The exigencies of the first (Maria's need to be significant) bring about the manipulations of the second, as though the text were trying to control its own meaning because its interpretation mattered to Maria.

Two theoretical points about desire will help to account for the peculiar "social" function of the narrator of "Clay" and for the phantasmal narrative voice. Human desire is always born out of an imaginary lack, and desire has another desire, or recognition, as its object. Maria's lacks are imaginary because, like everyone, as an organism she is a plenum, she has everything sufficient for life, and the things she lacks (marriage, wealth, class, beauty) exist only symbolically, in the significance they have for her: a significance itself grounded in their desirability to others. It is in the way sexual attributes become socially codified and significant—the way the difference between male and female, sexually active and celibate, fertile and barren, for example, becomes ontologically as well as semiotically significant within the symbolic order of her society—that Maria, as old maid, is caused especially to suffer. In her social world, being an unmarried, childless, and virginal woman endows her with a negative prestige whose consequences are encoded even in something as trivial as a card game that treats the Old Maid as the nightmare image of undesirability, whose visitation is greeted with dread and disgust as though she could spread her negativity, her status as loser, to all she touches. In fact, Maria plays a different children's game in "Clay": a game of divination that foretells the future life of young virgins (Ellmann), a future whose state-of-life symbols (ring and prayer book, e.g.) express the semiology of sexually marked and unmarked states. Maria's inappropriate inclusion in the game—she is, after all, an adult and she already has a life—betrays the way a sexually unmarked life, a life negatively marked as virginal, is treated by her society as a life perpetually deferred.

The symptoms the old maid's lacks produce are therefore not solitary brooding and depression but social strategies designed to capture significance by winning the approval of the "other." This theoretical background helps explain our sense that, although "Clay" is narrated in the third person, the speaker is really Maria. I would formulate it this way: narrative speech in "Clay" is mostly uttered in the language of Maria's desire; it is Maria's desire speaking. And because the narration functions to restore significance to Maria, it preserves the triangular structure of an eavesdropped conversation: the narrative voice of "Clay" describes Maria as she would like to catch someone speaking about her to someone else. Expressed differently, the narration is putatively directed toward us, to tell us about Maria, but its true beneficiary is Maria herself, whose prestige is certified by being "recognized" by objective and anonymous "others." If we were to construct a "narrator" from these functions, its personification would be an impossible social hybrid—a creature that is simultaneously Maria's social superior (like the authoritative and eloquent matron) and her metaphysical inferior (as loyally committed to her admiration and protection as the "vassals and serfs" of her song). This discrepancy undermines the narration on its errand for recognition. It it as though Maria sends us an inadequate signifier to extol her merits: a servant in the penetrable disguise of master. Her paltry stratagem, not the narrator, betrays Maria's ontological plight.

The distinctive features of the story's narration serve the function of gratifying Maria's desire for recognition. The rhetoric is shaped to restore to Maria, discursively, everything that might seem to constitute a "lack" for her—beauty, husband, children, home, wealth, status—albeit with the qualifications and feints of psychological realism. Restored, these things remain as imaginary as when they were "lacks," but they allow Maria to feel as if she possessed them, as if she enjoyed the security of wealth ("how much better it was to be independent and to have your own money in your pocket") and the affection of a family ("he had wanted her to go and live with them"); as if she had emotional, if not biological, children ("but Maria is my proper mother") and enough attractiveness for her purposes ("she found it a nice tidy little body"). These restorations create a version of Maria's condition that she presumably would like to believe but that the narration does not ultimately succeed in making tenable. According to this version, Maria is a well-bred, middle-class maiden lady living on a small but independent income from a job that earns her the respect of co-workers and superiors. Though unmarried and, of course, childless, she enjoys the affection of a surrogate family that had once employed her more as a governess than as a domestic and that still cherishes her as a favorite sort of godmother who visits them laden with gifts. This version of Maria's life is contradicted by a second, repressed version that is never articulated in the narrative speech but must be read in the narrative silences, ruptures, and evasions that lie between the lines, or in the margins of the text, so to speak, and that constitute the smudged and effaced portions of the "Clay" palimpsest. According to this second, unconscious version that she "knows" but does not "recognize," Maria works long hours for meager pay as a scullion in a laundry for reformed prostitutes who make her the butt of their jokes. She is ignored and patronized by everyone, including the family whose slavey she once was and from whom she succeeds in extorting only a minimal and ritualized tolerance by manipulating their guilt and pity. These intrinsically related versions are both psychically authored (but not authorized) by Maria. The first, positive version replaces and abolishes the second, whose "truth" about her insignificance Maria finds intolerable. It fails despite the inestimable advantage of being articulated in speech. Maria's fears can utter the negative version of her life only in silent semiologies: a wince, a blush, a lost object, a moment of forgetfulness, a mistake. The narration becomes a psychological mise-en-scène in which desire is attacked from within.

The drama that transpires within the narrative speech of "Clay" inevitably triggers a hermeneutical drama that fragments the reader into conflicting roles. Although I reify this reader as "we" in my discussion, I intend the plural to encompass not only the collectivity of actual readers but also the multiplicity of roles that the "reader" as a fictional construct of the story embodies: such roles as the gullible narratee, the skeptical critic, the self-reflexive metareader. "Clay" also uses the extent to which the reader has been historically constructed by novelistic convention. The story's narratee, for example—the putative listener who believes that Maria's life is simple, but good and admirable—embodies the ideology of a docile consumer of nineteenth-century narrative conventions. This interpretation reflects the fiction of Victorian fiction: that mousy governesses and plain dependents, the Jane Eyres and Esther Summersons, can become the heroes of their lives and stories by their everyday acts and virtues. But as discrepancies mount between what is said and what is shown, the reader's docile response is transformed into a critical gaze, hostile to Maria's desire and determined to see Maria not as she wishes to be seen but as she wishes not to be seen. This vision corresponds to the aims and methods of naturalism, as it exposes beneath bourgeois desire and delusion the occluded squalor and humiliation in the lives of the poor. Where the reader as narratee hears the testimonials of Maria's admiring co-workers, for example, the reader as critic sees old prostitutes amuse themselves at her expense. But Joyce subjects even this naturalistic "truth" to a final interrogative twist that causes the text to reflect the reader's smug superiority like a mirror. The reader's defection from the rhetorical program is coaxed, then implicitly judged. In the end, the reader of "Clay" is read by the text.

The reader's collusions with the narrative agenda are partly conditioned by the authority (and its erosion) of the narrative voice. "Clay" could not be narrated in the first person, by Maria herself, because if Maria is really as insignificant as she (unconsciously) believes, we would undoubtedly dismiss her flattering version of herself as empty boasting or wishful thinking. Furthermore, the narration makes us question whether Maria could speak for herself. She is, after all, quoted directly only in her reactive speech, as affirming or disclaiming the statements of others, *"Yes, my dear"* and *"No, my dear."* We do not know if her elided "actual" speech would possess the refinement of accent and diction required to convey the favorable impression that she seeks. It makes sense, therefore, to imagine Maria implicitly inventing, or wishing she could invent, someone who will speak for her (while pretending to speak of her) in the ways she cannot speak for herself. This narrator (the fictitious embodiment of such an invented or wished-for narrative voice) must therefore be rendered respectable, and to this end an important strategy in the arsenal of desire is produced: imitation. The narrative voice probably does not speak in the language of

Maria's class—whose diction cannot be verified from the text—but uses the idiom of someone mimicking the accents of respectable bourgeois folks, like the matron of the *Dublin by Lamplight* laundry—"so genteel." In this respect, the narration of "Clay" operates on Hugh Kenner's "Uncle Charles Principle," which "entails writing about someone much as that someone would choose to be written about." The word *conservatory,* used to name the place that houses Maria's plants, is borrowed from a social class that lives in mansions and marble halls rather than in laundries. The gentility of Maria's attitudes and opinions—with its optimistic accentuation of the positive ("she found it a nice tidy little body") and its polite circumlocutions ("how easy it was to know a gentleman even when he has a drop taken")—represents, if not the language of the bourgeoisie, then Maria's notion of both the sentiment and the phrasing of proper middle-class speech.

The narrative voice further buttresses its credibility by producing testimonials from witnesses in all strata of Maria's world to document her prestige. Strategically clustered at the beginning of the narration, in order to create a favorable first impression, these testimonials are curiously self-canceling because each tribute appears to depend on pushing aside an unpleasant reality in Maria's life. One of the laundry women, for example, inflates Maria's diplomatic skill by setting it in an implied climate of bullying and violence: "And Ginger Mooney was always saying what she wouldn't do to the dummy who had charge of the irons if it wasn't for Maria." The cook illustrates Maria's domestic skill by replacing with an aesthetic image ("the cook said you could see yourself in the big copper boilers") the grim visage of Maria's drudgery as she scours the pots to make them shiny. But the most prestigious testimonial comes from a witness in authority whose commendation is quoted verbatim—"One day the matron had said to her:—Maria, you are a veritable peace-maker!" Maria's peacemaking, the estimation of the matron, and the matron's fine vocabulary—"veritable"—are all paraded here, and any remaining skeptics are offered additional corroboration: "And the sub-matron and two of the Board ladies had heard the compliment." But not only does this lavish praise paradoxically draw attention to the chronic quarreling and dissension that seem to necessitate it; later narrative events sharply dispute these claims for the success of Maria's intervention by dramatizing just the opposite. Her meddling into the Donnelly brothers' quarrel nearly kindles a marital fight. We may hear of her peacemaking but we see these efforts prolong and multiply discord.

This complimentary prattle becomes exposed as empty words about the self that fill the space of Maria's insecurities as soon as we confront the censored blanks in the narrative discourse. The first of these occurs when a string of pleasantries about the *Dublin by Lamplight* laundry is punctured by a curious complaint: "There was one thing she didn't like and that was the tracts on the walls; but the matron was such a nice person to deal with, so genteel." The next creates a series of related enigmas about the laundry: that it has a puzzling religious and institutional orientation rather than a more logical commercial one and that pious Maria is inexplicably offended by a religious text on its walls. This informational gap clearly defines the story's narratee as a naïf, as someone whose ignorance about the true function of *Dublin by Lamplight* can be exploited to Maria's good account. In groping for a way to explain Maria's complaint, the narratee turns from the question of the laundry to the only difference that seems to signify: the difference between Catholic and Protestant. The complaint is interpreted as another of Maria's virtues, a theological virtue, no less, in the form of her Catholic orthodoxy affronted by Protestant Bible thumping. Only the reader armed with the knowledge that *Dublin by Lamplight* was a charitable institution for reformed prostitutes (Beck) can foil this narrative stratagem and discover what it conceals: that Maria knows the kind of place that is her home, that the tracts on the walls are a constant reminder of that fact—even if she could overlook the vulgarity and the violence of the women—that anyone who visits her at the laundry finds its status as a laundered whorehouse advertised on its walls. The narrative voice skillfully keeps the true purpose of the laundry a secret, while remarking, but disguising, Maria's discomfort with it.

A closer look at the semiotics of Maria's complaint brings its structure as a censored blank into even clearer focus. The laundry's scandal—the sexual promiscuity whose abolition is its premise—is communicated to us through a series of displaced negations or effacements. The narrator transforms us, in a sense, into a myopic or blind person, confronted by a wall we cannot see that contains writing we cannot read—although we are given to understand that the writing is there. If we could read it (as Reichert, Senn, and Zimmer hypothetically read the motto of *Dublin by Lamplight* laundry: 2 Timothy 2:26, "they recover themselves from the snare of the devil, to whose will they are held captive"), we would find in the text only the erasure of the vice, the bleaching of the stain, as it were, in the exhortation to reform that is the text's message. But we, as readers, can read all this only through the disapproval in Maria's eye as she gazes at walls we do not see.

The transitional passages that relate her journey from Ballsbridge to Drumcondra reflect an apparent narrational shift to accommodate a changing ontological perspective of Maria. The laundry and the Donnelly home represent sheltered interior spaces in which Maria appears to be socially encoded in flattering and affectionate terms as valued co-worker and dear family friend. But her journey thrusts Maria, anonymously and without credentials, into an outer world of crowded trams and frenetic shoppers in which she must make her way existentially, without the help of flattering testimonials. The narrative voice is obliged to adopt a seemingly existential mode in this section, relying on description as much as on interpretation and reporting action as much as attitude. This shift complicates the manipulation of the reader's favorable response and produces a set of self-correcting narrative maneuvers. While apparent objectivity lends the narration a particularly credible sound, it exerts itself no less in Maria's service. Whenever the narration cannot prevent us from catching glimpses of unflattering external perceptions of Maria, our attention is quickly diverted from the potentially critical eyes of strangers to Maria's laudable mental apparatus. For example, the determined objectivity of the report "The tram was full and she had to sit on the little stool at the end of the car, facing all the people, with her toes barely touching the floor" risks implying that the passengers might have found her pathetic sitting there "facing all the people," like a child on a dunce stool, and that she might have felt her conspicuous shortness ("her toes barely touching the floor") uncomfortably exposed. But the eyes of the strangers are occluded by a deft narrative move into Maria's mind, where we find no painful self-consciousness whatsoever as she busily tends her affairs ("She arranged in her mind all she was going to do"), cheers herself with happy anticipation, and weaves into homespun philosophy her concern over the Donnelly boys' fraternal quarrel: "but such was life."

It is not until we see Maria hopelessly dithering between two cake shops that we begin to suspect flaws and distractions in her putative mental composure. If on the tram she had already "arranged in her mind all she was going to do," why does she only now, when she has finished her shopping in Downes's cake shop, tackle her major decision of the evening, what treat to buy the Donnelly parents? Standing outside the shop, she begins her deliberations from scratch:

"Then she thought what else would she buy: she wanted to buy something really nice. They would be sure to have plenty of apples and nuts. It was hard to know what to buy and all she could think of was cake." Of course all she could think of was cake—having just come out of a cake shop after a protracted wait. A series of revisionist questions suggest themselves at this point. Was Maria distracted in her planning on the tram by the critical stare of the other passengers? Is it really the scanty icing on the Downes's plum cakes that prompts her to visit another shop, or is it her embarrassment and annoyance at having to reenter a shop that had served her rather tardily only moments before? Once she decides on plum cake, why does she vacillate so much in the Henry Street store that she earns a smart prod from the clerk? The narrative voice mentions only the stylish saleslady and Maria in the shop, but it does not say that they are alone. Is the shop crowded with customers who look on testily while Maria takes forever making her decision? I ask these questions to draw attention to the incompleteness and contradictoriness of what is narrated. The narrator's assertion of Maria's composure is often at odds with the depictions of her nervous and disorganized behavior, and the reader must decide whether to trust the narrative speech or the narrated gestures. However, notwithstanding the gaps that invite the investigation of the increasingly skeptical reader, the narrative voice still ably protects Maria from exposure at this point—covering even her self-betraying blush at the clerk's sarcastic wedding-cake reference with an elaborate courtship anecdote as the narration continues on the Drumcondra tram.

If the revisionist reading of the shopping incidents is produced entirely by the critical reader, the narration itself offers an *initial* version of what happened on the Drumcondra tram that is subsequently revised. In this way it exposes the first account, so flattering to Maria, to have functioned as a "lie." We may have earlier received the sense— through Maria's defensiveness ("she didn't want any ring or man either") and the revealing blush at the clerk's offer of wedding cake— that she suffers from a painful and humiliating sense of unmarriagability. The vignette on the tram, however, portrays her not only as pleasing enough to still attract the attentions of a distinguished ("colonel-looking") gentleman but also capable of entertaining his courtesies with perfectly well-bred ease and aplomb: she "favoured him with demure nods and hems" and "thanked him and bowed." His tipsiness is mentioned only as a trivial afterthought embedded in an exoneration: "she thought how easy it was to know a gentleman even when he has a drop taken." But later, when the forgotten plum cake is missed, we receive a different version of Maria's reaction, one that the narrative voice had, in fact, concealed from us: "Maria, remembering how confused the gentleman with the greyish moustache had made her, coloured with shame and vexation." This "confusion," along with the blush of remembrance it evokes, bears witness to a riot of hopeful, painful, uncontrollable feeling that erupts in Maria at every mention of the subject of marriage—a subject one had assumed was long ago serenely settled as outside her realm of plausibilities. We are now invited to recognize that the narrative prose, with its genteel accents, had been giving us the romantic distortions of Maria's desire: the wish to see in a fat flushed old drunk a courtly gentleman, whose military bearing is a metonymic expansion of a gray moustache and whose social imbibing ("when he has a drop taken") a synecdochic contraction of intemperate swilling.

It is important to ask why the narrative voice would tell us the "truth" about Maria's encounter with the colonel-looking gentleman after having troubled to conceal or censor just that fact in the first place. The answer is that the narration does not technically "lie" in the sense of deliberately concealing a known fact but rather exhibits the "blind spot" that is the epistemological consequence of desire. As we look for glorified images of ourselves in the admiring eyes of others, we fail to see ourselves as we are at that moment, as seekers of glorified self-reflections in others' eyes. Maria's narration is doomed to fail in its attempt to direct and control how others see her precisely because it has such a blind spot and cannot, therefore, entirely manipulate the truth about herself—or itself. Her narration cannot see itself as a language of desire, as it were: it cannot see the insecurities and fears that are its source. The forgotten plum cake catches both Maria and her narrative voice off guard and causes the narrative voice, shaken by Maria's discomposure, to blurt out a series of damaging revelations: Maria's hidden excitement on the tram, her urgent need to trade scant resources for goodwill ("At the thought of the failure of her little surprise and of the two and fourpence she had thrown away for nothing she nearly cried outright"), and her bad manners in moments of stress ("Then she asked all the children had any of them eaten it—by mistake, of course"). Preoccupied as it is with soothing Maria's distress, the narrative voice that earlier said too little now says, perhaps inadvertently, too much: "the children all said no and looked as if they did not like to eat cakes if they were to be accused of stealing." This important and prescient observation supplies the children's motive for their subsequent trick-or-treat-like reprisal against Maria. But the narration obscures the significance of the injured feelings of the children (who receive no apology from Maria and no sympathy from the narrative voice) by immediately turning to the attention lavished on Maria, who is plied with stout, nuts, and entertaining anecdotes—ostensibly to distract her from her loss. The narrative agenda here aims to establish Maria's privileged status in the Donnelly household, as it previously established Maria's privileged status in the laundry. The shadowy children—whose largely unspecified number, gender, and names indicate both Maria's and the narrator's lack of interest in them—are repressed like unpleasant thoughts. They behave accordingly, erupting in unexpected places and in devious ways. Although we never clearly see it there, their grievance is behind the disturbance in the game and it causes the narration to falter and nearly fragment. The narration recovers, however, without exposing Maria: "Maria understood that it was wrong that time and so she had to do it over again: and this time she got the prayer-book."

The gaps in the narration of the game are so sizable that the reader is obliged to reconstruct through elaborate inference both a scenario of what happens in the plot and an interpretation of what the events mean. Yet the critic who plunges into this talk without interrogating the reason for the gaps or questioning the function they serve risks being manipulated into narrative collusion. For example, Warren Beck, whose excellent reading of "Clay" I must admire, nonetheless duplicates the narrator's function of protecting Maria in the way he construes the game's disturbance. His reconstruction—that Mrs. Donnelly protects Maria from the shock of receiving the ill omen of "death within the coming year"—begs many questions. If "clay" is a traditional symbolic object in the game, they surely previous players have chosen it and survived, and it is neither taken seriously nor feared. Why must Maria, who is well and seemingly unconcerned with her mortality, be protected from the omen on this particular occasion? If the "clay" is a traditional part of the game, why does Maria not recognize it in the "soft wet substance" she touches and note, with satisfaction, Mrs. Donnelly's kindness in sparing her its meaning? There is nothing in Beck's explanation that the narrative voice, at least, could not report to us explicitly.

The narrative fracture of this episode makes sense only if there is something to hide, from Maria, and from us if we are to be maintained as appreciative narratees. I believe that the narration suppresses the causal link between the lost plum cake and the sabotaged game, a link in which the maligned children's reprisal takes the form of a trick that is itself an eruption of the "truth" of the children's true feelings; had it worked, it would have forced further involuntary self-betrayals from Maria. The children are coerced into attesting to Maria's generosity ("Mrs. Donnelly said it was too good of her to bring such a big bag of cakes and made all the children say:—Thanks, Maria") and are prevented from expressing their obvious dislike of her except through the veil of ambiguity. While the narrator nudges us to interpret *"O, here's Maria!"* as a joyful welcome, we can, in retrospect, hear it in the inaudible expletives and qualifications of resigned hostility and displeased surprise, as in *"O god, here's Maria already."* The prank with the garden dirt expresses and gratifies the Donnelly children's aggression toward Maria with minimal risk to themselves: it is perpetrated by the older next-door girls (presumably immune to punishment from the Donnelly parents), and it cunningly mitigates the pranksters' blame by manipulating the victim's own imagination in order to inflict shock and repulsion. For it strikes me as curious, if the "clay" is a symbolic object in the game, that Maria guesses neither what it means nor what it is made of. I believe that Maria is subjected to a much more primitive, conventional, universal childish trick, a trick that depends on making the victim mistake a neutral and benign substance (spaghetti, mushroom soup, Baby Ruth bars, in the game's American versions) for a repulsive, usually excretory material (worms, vomit, turds, etc.) The point of the children's joke is to make prim, "genteel" Maria recoil in shock and disgust at the sensation of touching "excrement"—only to reveal to her, on removal of the blindfold, the harmless garden dirt. The embarrassment would be self-inflicted: the victim would be betrayed by her own "dirty" mind.

The remarkable thing about the trick is not only that it fails, that Maria does not get it, but that a trick, as such, is never mentioned in the story at all, meaning that the narrative voice does not "get it" either:

> They led her up to the table amid laughing and joking and she put her hand out in the air as she was told to do. She moved her hand about here and there in the air and descended on one of the saucers. She felt a soft wet substance

with her fingers and was surprised that nobody spoke or
took off her bandage. There was a pause for a few seconds;
and then a great deal of scuffling and whispering. Somebody
said something about the garden, and at last Mrs. Donnelly
said something very cross to one of the next-door girls and
told her to throw it out at once: that was no play. Maria
understood that it was wrong that time and so she had to do
it over again; and this time she got the prayer-book.

This is narration under a blindfold. Like Maria's literal blindfold or
"bandage," the gap in the narration—the narrative voice's failure to
explain to us what really happened—represents, metaphorically, the
blind spot that marks the site of Maria's psychic wound, her imaginary
lacks and fears. For at issue here is more than Maria's failure to make
the connection between garden dirt and excrement. She dare not
recognize the trick itself, that a trick has been played on her, that she is
an object of ridicule, the butt of jokes, a person without sufficient
authority to restrain the pranks of malicious youngsters. What is
censored by the narration is the significance of what happens, and that
significance is the demonstration (once more) of Maria's fear of utter
insignificance. What Maria fears is not the touch of excrement on her
fingers but the recognition that her only "family"—like the rest of the
world—treats her like shit. This interpretation explains as well why the
word *clay* never appears in the story except as the title. The "soft wet
substance" in the narrative is never named, because the very ambiguity
of its identity is fraught with such cruel danger to Maria's ego. The
naming of the story poses a similar crux, a similar danger; the chosen
title, "Clay," therefore promises an interpretation of Maria's life that
preserves complex registers of truth telling and lying. For the narration
of "Clay" is "clay," in the sense that it is a polite circumlocution that
eradicates the dirt and squalor of Maria's life and thereby replicates her
own efforts as a slavey. "Clay" names and exhibits the work of a
rhetorical scullion.

Maria's song, her third task in the triadic fairy-tale structure of the
story, marks—like her earlier efforts of the gift and the game—an
unsuccessful social ritual, a failed attempt to govern her symbolic
relationships with others to her better advantage. Once again, there is
ambiguity in the request that she sing. We suspect that perhaps the
family asks Maria to sing less because her singing gives them pleasure
("Mrs. Donnelly bade the children be quiet and listen to Maria's

song") than because the request is an effective way to get rid of her, to hint that she has overstayed her welcome: "At last the children grew tired and sleepy and Joe asked Maria would she not sing some little song before she went." Maria responds on two levels to the double meanings of his request. Consciously, she fulfills the conventions of parlor performance by acting like a demure girl, feigning reluctance in order to extort coaxing (*"Do, please, Maria!"*) and delivering her song with blushing modesty. Unconsciously, she answers this extrusion from the Donnelly "family" with a song of exile—a song written in a language of desire even more explicit than that of "Clay." Maria chooses a song from an opera, *The Bohemian Girl,* that is itself a nearly perfect example of the infantile wish fantasy Freud called the "family romance": the child's fantasy that its parents are really imposters and that its "true" parents are royalty or aristocrats to whom the child will one day be restored. The prescience of Bunn's princess, abducted in infancy by gypsies but still able to divine her true estate ("I dreamt that I dwelt in marble halls / With vassals and serfs at my side"), nicely mirrors Maria's own implied sense of class displacement, of being trapped in a class below her breeding and sensibility ("she knew that Mooney meant well enough, of course, she had the notions of a common woman"). The song, another version of Maria's desire ex-pressed in the borrowed language of the superior class, is such a close analogue to the narration of "Clay" that Maria's lapsus, her omission of the verse depicting courtship and a marriage proposal, seems almost superfluous. but Joyce uses the specifically romantic content of Maria's repression (suitors, husband, love) to focus carefully the sexual etiol-ogy of her inferiority complex and to emphasize that it is not poverty alone but the negative symbolic value of being an old maid and being unloved that robs her of significance. Because the performance of the song operates on several semiological levels, it requires a complex act of decoding, and it is not clear, from the text, whether Joe listens to the song or to the singer. Does he hear the pathos of Maria's own plight in her song and weep for Maria, or—made maudlin by an excess of stout—is he moved to tears by the pain of the Bohemian girl ("What's Hecuba to him, or he to Hecuba, / That he should weep for her?" [*Hamlet* 2.2.559–60]) while he remains deaf to Maria's song of exile and longing?

When "Clay" ends—fittingly, with blindness and lost objects— what has been accomplished? "Clay" remains a hypothetical speech act, Maria's story as no one will ever tell it, as Maria could not even tell it herself, but as it might be imagined being told. For Maria, the story, far from remedying her lacks, has multiplied them, but not until they have passed through the detour of a flattering lie. But is the story, in its residual meaning, merely an exhibition of a pointless life, or is it the exhibition of the failure of Maria's denial of its pointlessness? It may seem to come to the same thing, but in the difference between a judgment (that Maria's life is pointless) and her failed resistance to that judgment is lodged that attitudinal half-turn away from Maria and toward the cad who does the judging. By producing Maria's interpretation, we are implicated in her estimation of herself, offering it as narratee and withdrawing it as critic, and we thereby contribute to her victimization. The naturalistic "truth" of her poverty and isolation, which we uncover by seeing "through" the narrative agenda, makes her life hard enough. But what disturbs her contentment with her lot and ruins the efficacy of a kind of Ibsenesque "life lie" are the insecurities produced by her fears of the estimation and interpretation of the "other." In her insecurities, in her fears, we should see our own "evil eye" as readers, encoded as we are within the story as the washerwomen, the shopkeepers, the young men on the tram, the children, and Society ("with a big ess," as Gerty MacDowell would say). It is we, as critical and perceptive readers, who create the pressures that necessitate Maria's defensive maneuvers in the way she invents her story.

I was myself prodded to make a self-reflexive turn when some of my students stubbornly refused to let me get away with an elision necessary to sustain my naturalistic reading of the story: what about the narrator's describing Maria (a mythical three times) in the unmistakably stereotyped features of a witch: "the tip of her nose nearly met the tip of her chin"? This description is indeed a problem, because surely the narrative voice does not flatter Maria here. Yet the voice and context in which the narration delivers these descriptions reveals a necessary concession fronted with the best possible "face," as it were, that one finds elsewhere in the story. Following the initial description of the kitchen—with its flattering signs of Maria's industry in its cleanliness, coziness, and orderliness—we receive a no-nonsense description of Maria's physical appearance: "Maria was a very, very small person indeed but she had a very long nose and a very long chin." This blunt and objective sentence is as eloquent in what it does not say as in what it does say. Neither the narrative voice nor any character in the story ever says or is described as thinking that Maria is plain or homely, deformed or grotesque looking, hideous or witchlike. Such interpretations, based strictly on the inferences of the reader, are hermeneutical, not rhetorical, products of the text. Indeed, the rhetoric of the description softens its sense in subtle ways. The description of Maria's stature, while quite emphatic in its "very, very small . . . indeed," nonetheless averts and replaces more evaluative judgments that would interpret her size as an abnormality or deformity and identify Maria as a dwarf or midget. By calling attention to her size and body first, as though they were her salient features, the narration also renders the more damaging information about her facial physiognomy less conspicuous; the curious syntax, with the "but" serving as a possible qualification, could even be read as a compensatory tribute, as though Maria's childish height were effectively countered by distinctive, well-marked adult features. I am suggesting here only that the narrative voice appears not to try to put a good face on Maria's face—not that it succeeds in flattering her.

During the tea, Maria twice produces the famous laugh in which "the tip of her nose nearly met the tip of her chin"—a laugh repeated later, a third time, at the Donnelly house, just as she is blindfolded for the game. Each of these occasions represents a moment of extraordinarily heightened, but uncomfortably ambiguous, attention to Maria: she is told she is sure to get the ring; a toast is drunk to her health with clattering tea mugs; the children insist on blindfolding her for the game. Is Maria being singled out for affectionate tribute, or is she being pressed into service—as dwarves and midgets historically were—as jester and fool? If the latter, does the narrative voice strategically use an uncharacteristically unflattering image of Maria to divert our attention from much more painful revelations? Does this rhetorical maneuver turn Maria from tormented buffoon into indulgent good sport ("she knew Mooney meant well, though, of course") and mask as jolly heartiness her grimace of pain? Does Lizzie Fleming twit and goad Maria nearly to tears about the ring, obliging the narrative voice gallantly to mask Maria's face at that painful moment with a most genteel turn of phrase—"when she laughed her grey-green eyes sparkled with disappointed shyness"? The narration has here produced another ambiguous scene whose possible interpretations hold the extremes of estimation for Maria: was the tea fun, was Maria made much of by people who love her, and did she express her pleasure in a grimace of hilarity, or was it a frequent ritual of cruel humiliation in which the aging prostitutes mock Maria's unlosable virginity?

Maria never sees that "the tip of her nose nearly met the tip of her chin" because the facial expression is, ironically, her most public gesture: her response to uncomfortable moments in the limelight when, perhaps terrified of the extreme exposure, she loses altogether her ability to compose herself. When she later looks at herself in the mirror, in the privacy of her room, she does not see her face at all; she sees only her body, as it looked when it was young and when, perhaps, its size was less conspicuous. She serenely approves what she sees—"In spite of its years she found it a nice tidy little body." If the narration shows us only Maria's contented acceptance of her appearance and does not disparage her nose and chin or show any character in the story disparaging them, why would a reader infer she is ugly and witchlike? With such a question the story turns itself on the reader like a mirror, a turn announced in the opening paragraph when "the cook said you could see yourself in the big copper boilers" and invited us to inspect our own visages in Maria's efforts to scour away the squalor of her life. Why do readers think Maria is ugly? A truthful reply returns an unflattering self-image to readers: that we possess, if our place in the symbolic order of our culture is a safe distance from its margins, a hermeneutical touch as poisonous as that of any witch who ever turned prince into toad. We take minute anatomical deviations—a few inches in height, a few centimeters extra on a nose or a chin—and pouf! we construct a witchlike hag that we expel from possibilities of desirability or estimation. "Clay" tricks us with the same trick the children try to play on Maria. It offers us a benign, neutral substance—a woman, just a woman—and we recoil with cries, or at least thoughts, of "witch!" as surely as we could recoil with cries of "shit!" from the harmless garden soil. "Clay" reads the reader when it implicity asks, "Which is the witch?"

Chronology

1882   James Augustine Aloysius Joyce born in Dublin on February 2 to John Stanislaus Joyce, tax-collector, and Mary Jane (May) Murray Joyce. He is the eldest of ten children who survive infancy, of whom the closest to him is his next brother Stanislaus (born 1884).

1888–91   Attends Clongowes Wood College, a Jesuit boarding school. He eventually is forced to leave because of his father's financial troubles. During Joyce's childhood and early adulthood, the family moves many times, from respectable suburbs of Dublin to poorer districts, as its size grows and its finances dwindle. Charles Stewart Parnell dies on October 6, the young Joyce writes an elegy, "Et tu, Healy." His father, a staunch Parnellite, has the poem printed, but no copies survive.

1892–98   Briefly attends the less intellectually prestigious Christian Brothers School, then attends Belvedere College, another Jesuit school.

1898–1902   Attends University College (also Jesuit); turns away from Catholicism and Irish nationalist politics. Writes a play, *A Brilliant Career* (which he later destroys), and essays, several of which are published. Graduates in 1902 with a degree in modern languages, having learned French, Italian, German, Norwegian, and Latin. Leaves Dublin to go to Paris and study medicine.

1903   Joyce works primarily on writing poems (which will be published in 1907 as *Chamber Music*) and reading Jonson at the Bibliothèque Ste. Geneviève. Receives a telegram from his father ("Mother dying come home Father"). Returns to Dublin, where May Joyce dies of cancer on August 13, four months after her son's return.

1904   An essay-narrative, "A Portrait of the Artist," is rejected for publication; several poems are published in various magazines, and a few stories, which eventually appear in *Dubliners*, are published. Stays for a time in the Martello Tower with Oliver St. John Gogarty (Malachi Mulligan in *Ulysses*). Joyce takes his first walk with Nora Barnacle on June 16 ("Bloomsday" in *Ulysses*). The daughter of a Galway baker, she is working in a Dublin boarding house. In October, Joyce and Nora leave for the continent, where they will live the remainder of their lives. Joyce finds work at a Berlitz school in Pola (now in Yugoslavia).

1905   The Joyces (as they are known, although they do not marry until 1931, for "testamentary" reasons) move to Trieste, where Joyce teaches at the Berlitz school. Birth of son Giorgio on July 27. Joyce submits manuscript of *Chamber Music* and *Dubliners* to Dublin publisher Grant Richards. Joyce's brother Stanislaus joins them in Trieste.

1907   After a year in Rome, where Joyce worked in a bank, the Joyces return to Trieste, where Joyce does private tutoring in English. *Chamber Music* published in London (not by Grant Richards). Birth of a daughter, Lucia Anna, on July 26. Writes "The Dead," the last of the stories that will become *Dubliners*. Works on revision of *Stephen Hero,* an adaptation of the essay "A Portrait of the Artist," later to be *A Portrait of the Artist as a Young Man*. Begins writing articles for an Italian newspaper.

1908   Abandons work on *Portrait* after completing three of five projected chapters.

1909   Joyce pays two visits to Dublin: in August, to sign a contract for the publication of *Dubliners* (not with Grant Richards), and in September as representative for a group who wish to set up the first cinema in Dublin. Returns to Trieste with sister Eva, who will now live with the Joyces.

1910   Cinema venture fails; publication of *Dubliners* delayed.

1911   Publication of *Dubliners* is held up, mainly because of what are feared to be offensive references to Edward

VII in "Ivy Day in the Committee Room." Joyce writes to George V to ask if he finds the story objectionable; a secretary replies that His Majesty does not express opinions on such matters.

1912   Final visit to Dublin with his family. Printer destroys the manuscript of *Dubliners*, deciding the book's aims are anti-Irish. Joyce takes the proofs of which he has gotten a copy from his equally unsympathetic publisher to London, but cannot find a publisher for them there, either.

1913   Joyce's original publisher, Grant Richards, asks to see the manuscript of *Dubliners* again. Ezra Pound, at the urging of William Butler Yeats, writes Joyce asking to see some of his work, since Pound has connections with various magazines, and might be able to help get Joyce published.

1914   Grant Richards publishes *Dubliners*. At Pound's urging, *A Portrait of the Artist as a Young Man* is published serially by the London magazine *The Egoist*. Joyce begins work on *Ulysses*. World War I begins on August 4.

1915   Joyce completes his play *Exiles*. After Joyce pledges neutrality to the Austrian authorities in Trieste who threatened to intern him, the family moves to Zürich, with the exception of Stanislaus, who is interned. Joyce awarded a British Royal Literary Fund grant, the first of several grants he will receive.

1916   Publishes *A Portrait of the Artist as a Young Man* in book form in New York.

1917   Undergoes the first of numerous eye operations.

1918   Grant Richards publishes *Exiles* in London; it is also published in the United States. The American magazine *The Little Review* begins serializing *Ulysses,* which is not yet complete. Armistice Day, November 11.

1919   Joyce refuses to be analyzed by Carl Jung. *The Egoist* also begins serializing *Ulysses*. The U.S. Post Office confiscates issues of *The Little Review* containing the "Lestrygonians" and the "Scylla and Charybdis" chapters.

1920–21   More issues of *The Little Review* confiscated. In September, John S. Sumner, the secretary of the New York Society for the Prevention of Vice, lodges a protest against the "Nausicaa" issue. The case comes to trial, and the *Review* loses, in February 1921. Publication ceases in the United States. Joyce and family move to Paris. Joyce finishes *Ulysses*. Sylvia Beach agrees to publish it in Paris.

1922   Shakespeare and Company, Sylvia Beach's press, publishes *Ulysses* in Paris on February 2, Joyce's birthday. Nora takes children to Galway for a visit, over Joyce's protests, and their train is fired upon by Irish Civil War combatants.

1923   Joyce begins *Finnegans Wake,* known until its publication as *Work in Progress.*

1924   Part of the *Work* appears in the Paris magazine *transatlantic review*.

1926   Pirated edition of *Ulysses* (incomplete) serialized in New York by *Two Worlds Monthly*.

1927   Shakespeare and Company publish *Pomes Penyeach*. Parts of *Work* published in Eugene Jolas's *transition,* in Paris.

1928   Joyce publishes parts of *Work* in New York to protect the copyright.

1929   Joyce assists at a French translation of *Ulysses,* which appears in February. Lucia Joyce's mental stability seems precarious. To his father's delight, Giorgio Joyce makes his debut as a singer, with some success.

1930   At Joyce's instigation, Herbert Gorman begins a biography of Joyce. Joyce supervises a French translation of *Anna Livia Plurabelle,* part of the *Work,* by Samuel Beckett and friends, which appears in the *Nouvelle Revue Française* in 1931. Marriage of son Giorgio to Helen Kastor Fleischman.

1931   Joyce marries Nora Barnacle at a registry office in London. Death of Joyce's father.

1932   Helen Joyce gives birth to a son, Stephen James, on February 15. Joyce writes "Ecce Puer," a poem celebrating the birth of his grandson. Daughter Lucia suffers first mental breakdown; she is diagnosed as hebephrenic (a form of schizophrenia). Bennett Cerf of Random House contracts for the American publication of *Ulysses*.

1933   On December 6, Judge John M. Woolsey admits *Ulysses* into the United States, declaring that "whilst in many

places the effect . . . on the reader undoubtedly is somewhat emetic, nowhere does it tend to be an aphrodisiac." Lucia Joyce hospitalized, as she will often be until
her permanent hospitalization.

1934   Random House publishes *Ulysses*.

1936   Publishes *Collected Poems* in New York, and *A Chaucer
A.B.C.* with illuminations by Lucia.

1939   *Finnegans Wake* published in London and New York.
War declared. The Joyces move to Vichy, France, to be
near Lucia's mental hospital.

1940   Herbert Gorman's authorized biography of Joyce appears. After the fall of France, the Joyces manage once
more to get to Zürich.

1941   Joyce dies following surgery on a perforated ulcer on
January 13. He is buried in Fluntern Cemetery, in
Zürich, with no religious ceremony, at Nora's request.

1951   Nora Barnacle Joyce dies in Zürich on April 10. She is
buried in Flutern as well, but not next to Joyce, since
that space has been taken. In 1966, the two bodies are
reburied together.

Contributors

HAROLD BLOOM, Sterling Professor of the Humanities at Yale University, is the author of *The Anxiety of Influence, Poetry and Repression,* and many other volumes of literary criticism. His forthcoming study, *Freud: Transference and Authority,* attempts a full-scale reading of all of Freud's major writings. A MacArthur Prize Fellow, he is general editor of five series of literary criticism published by Chelsea House. During 1987–88, he served as Charles Eliot Norton Professor of Poetry at Harvard University.

ROBERT ADAMS DAY is Professor of English and Comparative Literature at Queens College and the Graduate Center, City University of New York. He is the author of *Told in Letters: Epistolary Fiction Before Richardson* and "Joyce's Waste Land and Eliot's Unknown God."

TILLY EGGERS teaches at the University of Wyoming.

PHILLIP HERRING is Professor of English at the University of Wisconsin, Madison. He has written a number of articles on Joyce and edited *Joyce's Notes and Early Drafts for* Ulysses: *Selections from the Buffalo Collection* and *Joyce's* Ulysses *Notebooks in the British Museum.*

MARY T. REYNOLDS is the author of *Joyce and Dante: The Shaping Imagination.*

HUGH KENNER, Professor Emeritus of English at The Johns Hopkins University, is the leading critic of the High Modernists (Pound, Eliot, Joyce) and of Beckett. His books include *The Pound Era, The Stoic Comedians, Dublin's Joyce,* and *Ulysses.*

JOHN PAUL RIQUELME is Professor of English at Southern Methodist University and is the author of *Teller and Tale in Joyce's Fiction: Oscillating Perspectives* and the translator for Fritz Senn's *Joyce's Dislocations.*

LINDSEY TUCKER, who is Assistant Professor of English at Temple University, has written articles on Iris Murdoch, Frank Tuohy, and Joseph Heller and has published *Stephen and Bloom at Life's Feast: Alimentary Symbolism and the Creative Process in James Joyce's* Ulysses.

ROSS CHAMBERS is Professor of French at the University of Michigan. In addition to many articles, he has written *Story and Situation: Narrative Seductions and the Power of Fiction.*

FRITZ SENN, a Swiss scholar, has worked on Joyce for many years and has published articles on him in several languages. He is affiliated with *A Wake Newslitter* and the *James Joyce Quarterly*. A Collection of his essays has been edited under the title *Joyce's Dislocations: Essays on Reading as Translation*. He is currently head of the Zurich Joyce Foundation.

MARGOT NORRIS is Professor of English at the University of Michigan. She is the author of *The Decentered Universe of* Finnegans Wake and *Beasts of the Modern Imagination: Darwin, Nietzsche, Kafka, Ernst, and Lawrence.*

Bibliography

Baker, James R., and Thomas F. Staley, eds. *James Joyce's* Dubliners: *A Critical Handbook*. Belmont, Calif.: Wadsworth, 1969.

Beck, Warren. *Joyce's* Dubliners: *Substance, Vision and Art*. Durham, N.C.: Duke University Press, 1969.

Beja, Morris. "One Good Look at Themselves: Epiphanies in *Dubliners*." In *Work in Progress: Joyce Centenary Essays*, edited by R. F. Peterson et al., 3–14. Carbondale: Southern Illinois University Press, 1983.

———, ed. *James Joyce, "Dubliners" and "A Portrait of the Artist as a Young Man": A Selection of Critical Essays*. London: Macmillan, 1973.

Benstock, Bernard. "Joyce's Rheumatics: The Holy Ghost in *Dubliners*." *Southern Review* 14 (January 1978): 1–15.

———. "Text, Sub-Text, Non-Text: Literary and Narrational In/Validities." *James Joyce Quarterly* 22 (1985): 355–65.

Bogorad, Samuel N. "Gabriel Conroy as 'Whited Sepulchre': Prefiguring Imagery in 'The Dead.'" *Ball State University Forum* 14, no. 1 (1973): 52–58.

Bowen, Zack. "Joyce's Prophylactic Paralysis: Exposure in *Dubliners*." *James Joyce Quarterly* 19 (Spring 1982): 257–74.

Boyd, John D., and Ruth A. Boyd. "The Love Triangle in Joyce's 'The Dead.'" *University of Toronto Quarterly* 42 (Spring 1973): 202–17.

Boyle, Robert, S.J. "Swiftian Allegory and Dantean Parody in Joyce's 'Grace.'" *James Joyce Quarterly* 7 (Fall 1969): 11–21.

———. "'Two Gallants' and 'Ivy Day in the Committee Room.'" *James Joyce Quarterly* 1 (1963): 3–9.

Brandabur, Edward. *A Scrupulous Meanness*. Urbana: University of Illinois Press, 1971.

Brivac, Sheldon. *Joyce the Creator*. Madison: University of Wisconsin Press, 1985.

Brown, Homer Obed. *James Joyce's Early Fiction*. Cleveland: The Press of Case Western Reserve University, 1972.

Brown, Richard. *James Joyce and Sexuality*. Cambridge: Cambridge University Press, 1985.

Burgess, Anthony. *Joysprick: An Introduction to the Language of James Joyce*. London: André Deutsch, 1973.

Carrier, Warren. "*Dubliners*: Joyce's Dantean Vision." *Renascence* 17 (1965):211–15.

Chadwick, Joseph. "Silence in 'The Sisters.'" *James Joyce Quarterly* 21 (Spring 1984): 245–56.

Cixous, Helene. *The Exile of James Joyce.* Translated by Sally A. J. Purcell. New York: David Lewis, 1972.

———. "Joyce: The (R)use of Writing." In *Post-structuralist Joyce: Essays from the French,* edited by Derek Attridge and Daniel Ferrer, 15–30. Cambridge: Cambridge University Press, 1984.

Chambers, Ross. *Story and Situation.* Minneapolis: University of Minnesota Press, 1984.

Collins, Ben L. "Joyce's Use of Yeats and Irish History: A Reading of 'A Mother.'" *Eire-Ireland* 5 (Spring 1970): 45–66.

Connolly, Thomas E. "Joyce's 'The Sisters': A Pennyworth of Snuff." *College English* 27 (December 1965): 189–95.

Cope, Jackson I. "An Epigraph for *Dubliners.*" *James Joyce Quarterly* 7 (1970): 362–64.

Crawford, Claudia. "James Joyce's 'The Sisters': A Letter-L-Analysis." *American Imago* 41 (Summer 1984): 181–200.

Delany, Paul. "Joyce's Political Development and the Aesthetic of *Dubliners.*" *College English* 34 (November 1972): 256–66.

Dilworth, Tom. "Sex and Politics in 'The Dead.'" *James Joyce Quarterly* 23 (Winter 1986): 157–171.

Ellman, Richard. *The Consciousness of Joyce.* Toronto and New York: Oxford University Press, 1977.

———. *James Joyce.* Oxford: Oxford University Press, 1982.

Engle, Monroe. "*Dubliners* and Erotic Expectation." In *Twentieth-Century Literature in Retrospect,* edited by Reuben A. Brower, 3–26. Cambridge, Mass.: Harvard University Press, 1971.

Fabian, David R. "Joyce's 'The Sisters': Gnomon, Gnomic, Gnome." *Studies in Short Fiction* 5 (Winter 1968): 187–89.

Feeley, John. "Joyce's 'The Dead' and the Browning Quotation." *James Joyce Quarterly* 20 (Fall 1982): 87–96.

Feshbach, Sidney. "Writ Our Bit as Intermidgets: Classical Rhetoric in the Early Writing of James Joyce." *James Joyce Quarterly* 17 (Summer 1980): 379–87.

Foster, John W. "Passage through 'The Dead.'" *Criticism* 15 (Spring 1973): 91–108.

French, Marilyn. "Joyce and Language." *James Joyce Quarterly* 19 (Spring 1982): 443–73.

———. "Missing Pieces in Joyce's *Dubliners.*" *Twentieth Century Literature* 24 (Winter 1978): 443–73.

Friedrich, Gerhard. "The Gnomonic Clue to Joyce's *Dubliners.*" *MLN* 72 (1957): 421–24.

Garrett, Peter, ed. *Twentieth-Century Interpretations of "Dubliners": A Collection of Critical Essays.* Englewood Cliffs, N.J.: Prentice-Hall, 1968.

Gifford, Don. *Joyce Annotated.* Berkeley: University of California Press, 1982.

———. *Notes for Joyce:* Dubliners *and* A Portrait of the Artist as a Young Man. New York: Dutton, 1976.

Going, William T. "Joyce's Gabriel Conroy and Robert Browning: The Cult of 'Broadcloth.' " *Papers on Language and Literature* 13 (1977): 202–7.

Golding, S. L. "The Artistry of *Dubliners*." In *Twentieth Century Interpretations of Dubliners*, edited by Peter K. Garrett. Englewood Cliffs, N.J.: Prentice-Hall, 1968.

Hart, Clive, ed. *James Joyce's* Dubliners. London: Faber & Faber, 1969.

Hodgart, Matthew. *James Joyce: A Student's Guide.* London: Routledge & Kegan Paul, 1978.

Horowitz, Sylvia Huntley. "More Christian Allegory in 'Ivy Day in the Committee Room.' " *James Joyce Quarterly* 21 (Winter 1984): 145–54.

Joyce, Stanislaus. "The Background to *Dubliners*." *The Listener,* 25 March 1954: 526–27.

Kain, Richard M. "Grace." In *James Joyce's* Dubliners, edited by Clive Hart, 134–52. London: Faber & Faber, 1969.

Kain, Richard M. and Magalaner, Marvin. *Joyce: The Man, the Work, the Reputation.* New York: Collier, 1956.

Kelleher, John V. "Irish History and Mythology in James Joyce's 'The Dead.' " *The Review of Politics* 27 (July 1965): 414–33.

Kenner, Hugh. *"Dubliners."* In *Twentieth Century Interpretations of* Dubliners, edited by Peter K. Garrett, 38–56. Englewood Cliffs, N.J.: Prentice-Hall, 1968.

———. *Joyce's Voices.* Berkeley and Los Angeles: University of California Press, 1978.

Kibodeaux, R. Bruce. " 'Counterparts'—*Dubliners* without End." *James Joyce Quarterly* 14 (1976): 87–92.

Lachtmann, Howard. "Joyce's Ecclesiastical Satire in *Dubliners*." *James Joyce Quarterly* 7 (1970): 82–92.

Lodge, David. *The Modes of Modern Writing.* Ithaca, N.Y.: Cornell University Press, 1977.

Lucente, Gregory L. "Encounters and Subtexts in 'The Dead': A Note on Joyce's Narrative Technique." *Studies in Short Fiction* 20 (Fall 1983): 281–87.

Lyons, J. B. "Animadversions on Paralysis as Symbol in 'The Sisters.' " *James Joyce Quarterly* 11 (Spring 1974): 257–65.

MacCabe, Colin. *James Joyce and the Revolution of the Word.* London: MacMillan, 1978.

Magalaner, Marvin. *Time of Apprenticeship: The Fiction of Young James Joyce.* London: Abelard-Schulman, 1959.

———. "Joyce, Nietzsche, and Hauptmann in James Joyce's 'A Painful Case.' " *PMLA* 68 (March 1953): 95–102.

Mandel, Jerome. "Medieval Romance and the Structure of 'Araby.' " *James Joyce Quarterly* 13 (Winter 1976): 234–37.

Manganiello, Dominic. *Joyce's Politics.* London: Routledge & Kegan Paul, 1980.

Morrissey, L. J. "Joyce's Revision of 'The Sisters' from Epicleti to Modern Fiction." *James Joyce Quarterly* 24 (Fall 1986): 33–54.

Munich, Adrienne Auslander. "Form and Subtext in Joyce's 'The Dead.' " *Modern Philology* 82 (November 1984): 173–84.

Nilsen, Kenneth. "Down Among the Dead: Elements of Irish Language and Mythology in James Joyce's *Dubliners*." *Canadian Journal of Irish Studies* 12 (June 1986): 12–34.

O'Brien, Darcy. *The Conscience of James Joyce*. Princeton: Princeton University Press, 1968.

Owens, Coilin. " 'A Man With Two Establishments to Keep Up': Joyce's Farrington." *Irish Renaissance Annual* 4 (1983): 128–56.

Parrinder, Patrick. *Dubliners*. Cambridge: Cambridge University Press, 1984.

Pecora, Vincent D. " 'The Dead' and the Generosity of the Word." *PMLA* 101 (March 1986): 233–45.

Peake, C. H. *James Joyce: The Citizen and the Artist*. Stanford: Stanford University Press, 1977.

Rabate, Jean-Michel. "Silence in *Dubliners*." In *James Joyce: New Perspectives*, edited by Colin MacCabe, 45–72. Sussex: The Harvester Press. Bloomington: Indiana University Press, 1982.

Reichert, Klaus, Fritz Senn, and Dieter Zimmer, eds. *Materialien zu James Joyces* Dubliners. Frankfurt am Main: Suhrkamp, 1977.

Reid, Stephen. " 'The Beast in the Jungle' and 'A Painful Case': Two Different Sufferings." *American Imago* 20 (1963): 221–39.

Reynolds, Mary T. *Joyce and Dante: The Shaping Imagination*. Princeton: Princeton University Press, 1981.

Riquelme, John Paul. *Teller and Tale in Joyce's Fiction*. Baltimore: The Johns Hopkins University Press, 1983.

San Juan, Epifanio. *James Joyce and the Craft of Fiction: An Interpretation of* Dubliners. Rutherford, N.J.: Farleigh Dickinson University Press, 1972.

Scholes, Robert. "Further Observations on the Text of *Dubliners*." *Studies in Bibliography* 17 (1964): 107–24.

Scholes, Robert, and A. Walton Litz, eds. *"Dubliners": Text, Criticism, and Notes*. New York: Viking, 1967.

Scott, Bonnie Kime. *Joyce and Feminism*. Bloomington: Indiana University Press; Sussex: Harvester Press, 1984.

Senn, Fritz. "Dogmad or Dubliboused?" *James Joyce Quarterly* 17 (1980): 237–62.

———. " 'He Was Too Scrupulous Always': Joyce's 'The Sisters.' " *James Joyce Quarterly* 2 (Winter 1965): 66–72.

Shurgot, Michael W. "Windows of Escape and the Death Wish in Man: Joyce's 'The Dead.' " *Eire-Ireland* 17, no. 4 (1982): 58–71.

Staley, Thomas F. "A Beginning: Signification, Story and Discourse in Joyce's 'The Sisters.' " *Genre* 12 (Winter 1979): 533–49.

Stein, William Bysshe. " 'Counterparts': A Swine Song." *James Joyce Quarterly* 1 (1964): 30–32.

Stern, Frederick C. " 'Parnell is Dead': 'Ivy Day in the Committee Room.' " *James Joyce Quarterly* 10 (Winter 1973): 228–39.

Theoharis, Theoharis C. "*Heda Gabler* and 'The Dead.' " *English Literary History* 50 (Winter 1983): 791–810.

Tindall, William York. *A Reader's Guide to James Joyce*. New York: Noonday, 1959.

Torchiana, Donald T. *Backgrounds for Joyce's* Dubliners. Boston: Allen & Unwin, 1986.

———. "The Ending of 'The Dead': I Follow Saint Patrick." *James Joyce Quarterly* 18 (1981): 122–32.

———. "Joyce's 'Two Gallants': A Walk through the Ascendency." *James Joyce Quarterly* 6 (1968): 115–27.

———. "The Opening of *Dubliners:* A Reconsideration." *Irish University Review* 1 (1971): 149–60.

Voelker, Joseph C. " 'He Lumped the Emancipates Together': More Analogues for Joyce's Mr. Duffy." *James Joyce Quarterly* 18 (Fall 1980): 23–34.

Waisbren, Burton A., and Florence L. Walzl. "Paresis and the Priest: James Joyce's Symbolic Use of Syphilis in 'The Sisters.' " *Annals of Internal Medicine* 80 (June 1974): 758–62.

Walzl, Florence L. "A Book of Signs and Symbols: The Protaganist." In *The Seventh of Joyce,* edited by Bernard Benstock, 117–23. Bloomington: Indiana University Press, 1982.

———. *"Dubliners."* In *A Companion to Joyce Studies,* edited by Zack Bowen and James F. Carens, 157–228. Westport, Conn.: Greenwood, 1984.

———. *"Dubliners:* Women in Irish Society." In *Women in Joyce,* edited by Suzette Henke and Elaine Unkeless, 31–56. Urbana: University of Illinois Press, 1982.

———. "Gabriel and Michael: The Conclusion of 'The Dead.' " *James Joyce Quarterly* 4 (1964): 17–31.

———. "Joyce's 'Clay': Fact and Fiction." *Renascence* 35 (Winter 1983): 119–37.

———. "Joyce's 'The Sisters': A Development." *James Joyce Quarterly* 10 (Summer 1973): 375–421.

———. "The Life Chronology of *Dubliners.*" *James Joyce Quarterly* 14 (Summer 1977): 408–15.

———. "Patterns of Paralysis in Joyce's *Dubliners.*" *College English* 21 (1961): 221–28.

Acknowledgments

"Joyce's Gnomons, Lenehan, and the Persistence of an Image" by Robert Adams Day from *Novel: A Forum on Fiction* 14, no. 1 (Fall 1980), © 1980 by Novel Corp. Reprinted by permission.

"What Is a Woman . . . a Symbol Of?" by Tilly Eggers from *James Joyce Quarterly* 18, no. 4 (Summer 1981), © 1981 by the University of Tulsa. Reprinted by permission of the publisher.

"Structure and Meaning in Joyce's 'The Sisters' " by Phillip Herring from *The Seventh of Joyce*, edited by Bernard Benstock, © 1982 by Indiana University Press. Reprinted by permission of Indiana University Press and the Harvester Press Ltd.

"The Dantean Design of Joyce's *Dubliners*" by Mary T. Reynolds from *The Seventh of Joyce*, edited by Bernard Benstock, © 1982 by Indiana University Press. Reprinted by permission of Indiana University Press and the Harvester Press Ltd.

"Berlitz Days" by Hugh Kenner from *Renascence: Essays on Values in Literature* 35, no. 2 (Winter 1983), © 1983 by Marquette University Press. Reprinted by permission.

"Metaphors of the Narration / Metaphors in the Narration: 'Eveline' " by John Paul Riquelme from *Teller and Tale in Joyce's Fiction: Oscillating Perspectives* by John Paul Riquelme, © 1983 by the Johns Hopkins University Press, Baltimore/ London. Reprinted by permission of the Johns Hopkins University Press.

"Duffy's Last Supper: Food, Language, and the Failure of Integrative Processes in 'A Painful Case' " by Lindsey Tucker from *Irish Renaissance Annual IV*, edited by Zack Bowen, © 1983 by Associated University Presses, Inc. Reprinted by permission of Associated University Presses, Inc.

"Gabriel Conroy Sings for His Supper, or Love Refused ('The Dead')" by Ross Chambers from *Story and Situation: Narrative Seduction and the Power of Fiction*, © 1984 by the University of Minnesota. Reprinted by permission of the University of Minnesota Press.

" 'The Boarding House' Seen as a Tale of Misdirection" by Fritz Senn from *James Joyce Quarterly* 23, no. 4 (1986), © 1986 by the University of Tulsa. Reprinted by permission of the publisher.

" 'Ivy Day in the Committee Room': The Use and Abuse of Parnell" by Thomas B. O'Grady from *Eire-Ireland: A Journal of Irish Studies* 21, no. 2 (1986), © 1986 by *Eire-Ireland*, St. Paul, Minnesota 55105. Reprinted by permission of the Irish American Cultural Institute.

"Narration under a Blindfold: Reading Joyce's 'Clay' " by Margot Norris from *PMLA* 102, no. 2 (March 1987), © 1987 by the Modern Language Association of America. Reprinted by permission of the Modern Language Association of America.

Index